PIETRO BONOMETTI

CREMONA

A town worth discovering

The chapter «The tradition of stringed-instrument making»
is by:
MARCO TIELLA

edizioni
ITALCARDS
Modena Italy

Photos: *EZIO QUIRESI*
GIUSEPPE MUCHETTI
NOVAFOTO di PIETRO DIOTTI
CARLO CAPURSO (nature photograph)

ITALCARDS editions, Modena - Italy

The town's origins

A visitor who has come to the big Piazza del Duomo (Cathedral Square) by way of one of the twelve streets which converge there in a sunburst arrangement will perhaps not be aware of being on the town's highest point, i.e. 47 metres above sea level. This exact piece of information may seem mere pedantry, but the first Roman «castrum», on which the following settlements stratified, rose most probably on this very area which juts out like a projection — if we assume that the toponym Cremona, coming probably from a Celtic root, has the meaning of «projection».

In spite of the efforts of some local historians, however, it is still not possible to locate the crossing point between the «Cardo maximus» and the «Decumanus», the two main arteries which divided the Roman camp in the form of a cross. Nonetheless, if one goes across the Piazza and stops at the beginning of via Solferino he will see, below the present road level, significant remains of a Roman road with its massive and regular paving. This road portion was discovered in 1967 together with another one perpendicular to the first. However, this is too vague an indication to enable us to locate the crossing of the two arteries on that spot or not far from it. What is undoubted is that the first Roman camp, limited with meticulous regularity by the land surveyor and divided into a number of «insulae» (isles) by parallel roads arranged at right angles, must not have been very far from the Piazza. The present network of streets around the big Cathedral Square suggests the probable arrangement of the blocks of houses («insulae») around the centre of the «castrum». However, although the size of the first camp is more to be guessed at than ascertained, it is evident that the area where the beautiful Romanesque Cathedral now stands marks the extreme end of that projection, beyond which no development of the camp can be hypothesized. One thing is certain: where the present via Plàtina and the small Boccaccino square form a wide bend passing quite close to the Bishop's Palace and the three apses of the Cathedral the road level is sensibly lower than the square and increases gradually as streets depart from the town centre. In spite of this observation it is still not easy to find out whether the first Christian settlement was close to or just inside the boundaries of the Roman citadel. Now, if we consider that the area stretching below the projection was a marshy ground and if we look at the same flat area as a connection between the Roman town and the Postumia Way we are inclined to believe that the first early Christian building may have been raised on a place very close to the Roman camp. The steep slope helps us to understand why this eastern part of the town is still crossed by streets converging to Mosa Gate, whose name comes from the «mosii» i.e. the bogs created by the frequent floods of the Po river. Although the «Mosa» toponym was introduced in a more recent period than the events we are discussing, it suggests nonetheless that in ancient times the big river, which gives its name to Italy's biggest plain, could even reach the foot of this low projection on which, during the Middle Ages, the Cathedral was built.

Yet one of the most vexed questions is about the first evangelization of Cremona. According to tradition the first apostle of the town was Barnaba who, on his way from Rome to Milan, allegedly stopped in Florence and Cremona during his journey on the Cassia Way. Others speak of Sabino, appointed bishop in the year 55, while some other scholars, more cautiously, date back the origins of the Diocese of Cremona to Stephen, elected in 320. Even if the mention of apostle Barnaba, who travelled together with St.Paul, is far from being reliable, it would indeed explain the desire of the Cremona Diocese to claim for itself renowned origins when, in 1228, it came again under the Milan district after a temporary breaking away. As for Barnaba's successors it will be enough to mention a well-known historical phenomenon according to which the first bishops

---

Coat of arms of Cremona, once on top of Porta Romana (Roman Gate), which was demolished at the beginning of our century; today it is placed under the portico of the Loggia dei Militi (Soldiers' Loggia).

were not prelates of the Diocese but the most popular and revered Saints later included in the chronology of Bishops. What is certain is that the first reliable information about the history of the Cremona Diocese dates back to the middle of the 5th century.

The finding of a mosaic floor under the courtyard of the Torrazzo, very close to the small external apse of the Chapel of the Holy Thorn in the first decades of the 20th century, takes on therefore a significant importance. According to a reliable hypothesis the floor did not belong to a private house, as previously thought, but to a public building; in addition it seems that the important archaeological finding was realized at the end of the 4th century, that is to say in the early-Christian age. However, as we cannot determine the exact function of the room to which it belonged, we must be satisfied with a mere recording of the fact without trying to impose a forced interpretation — even if to suggest that the mosaic fragment could come from the remains of a Baptistry, a Basilica or another place of worship would be a charming hypothesis. If on the one hand the finding of gravestones with sepulchral inscriptions inside the area where now the Cathedral stands reminds us of the fact that Roman tombs were lined up along the streets departing from town, because Roman Law prohibited both cremation and burial inside the town walls,

on the other it suggests that this place may have been used as a sacred building since the beginning of the Christian age. Imperial Diplomas from the 9th-10th century mention only the existence of two churches devoted to St.Mary and St.Stephen. This is not at all unusual for Cremona. As for the old group of buildings of St.Lawrence, not far from the Cathedral, Bishop Olderico mentioned two nearby churches, the former devoted to St.Lawrence and the latter to St.Mary and the Apostles Philip and James, in the donation of a vaste expanse of land to the Benedictines in 986. Now, although the absence of documents and significant findings does not allow to have a clear image of the building or buildings which preceded the construction of the Cathedral in 1107, the two old sacred buildings devoted to St.Mary and St.Stephen erected close to the projection are to be considered as dating back to an earlier than the one of the Romanesque Cathedral, of which they were the forerunners. A new element is added to our knowledge. In a document dated 902 a «munitiuncula» (small stronghold) is mentioned among the possessions of the Bishop. The size of this citadel could approximately correspond to the

1. Piazza del Comune.
2. Façade of the Cathedral.
3. Aerial view of the historical town centre.

3

area which lies now behind the Cathedral and the Bishop's Palace and is marked by via Plàtina and the small Boccaccino Square. It has been rightly observed that the plan of the «munitiuncula» corresponded therefore to the town itself and that it was not changed even when Count-Bishop Landolfo was expelled from the town and the small fortress partly demolished.

Landolfo was later readmitted to the Bishop's seat and the citadel rebuilt and enlarged between 1027 and 1030. However occasional the Cremonese artistic production of that period may have been, there are documents reporting of an intense building activity during which the Count-Bishop took care in 1107 of the Church of St.Michael Vetere and the Benedictines were eager at governing St.Lawrence Church. In addition St.Victor Church, now destroyed, was rebuilt (1020), the Church of St.Peter upon Po was built

(1064) and the church and monastery devoted to the Saints Silvester and Benedict were initiated.

Finally, in the period of its highest splendour as a City State, the whole town of Cremona began in 1107 the construction of the Cathedral on the place where once the churches devoted to St.Mary and St.Stephen had stood. A late document preserved in the «Historiae» by Giovanni Balistario and mentioned during a controversy between Bishop Nicolò Sfondrati and the General Council of the Cremona Commune about the proprietorship of the Cathedral, the Torrazzo and the Baptistry, states that «when the Town of Cremona began to build the Church of Our Lady of the Assumption it was 1107». A much more precious document, however, now preserved over the entrance door to the Sacristy of the Canons, is the *foundation stone of the Cathedral*. **The Prophets Enoc and Elijah**, with a harshness which

already foretells a motion suppleness of motions and a plastic flexuosity which were hardly ever seen after the loss of classical modules, hold the slab on which the construction opening date is carved: **26 August 1107**. The historian Giuseppe Bresciani recalled that this precious piece was «at the head of the choir», while more recently other local historians have claimed that it was placed on the original altar, as it happened several centuries later for the first stone of St.Sigismund Church.

A dramatic piece of news is reported by the laconic records of the «Cremona Annals», written at the beginning of the 13th century: «...when the 1116 earthquake occurred — it was actually 3 January 1117 because, according to an old tradition, the year began then on 25 March — during the octave of St.John Evangelist at the Vespers». The Po valley was struck by an earthquake which badly damaged a number of sacred and profane buildings. The Cathedral of Modena resisted to the earth tremors thanks to its massive structure and it became later a model for the reconstruction works of many Cathedrals. Parma raised its new Cathedral followed by Piacenza whose new Cathedral was begun in 1122 and ended only in 1233. After Parma and Piacenza, Cremona also wanted a big Cathedral. In 1129, when the bones

of St.Imerio were found under the ruins, as reported by Bishop Sicardo, the building site became intensively active again, although it is now hard to fix a precise chronology of works after that date.

In his huge work written in 1971 about the Cathedral of Cremona, a local historian suggests among other things several graphic solutions for an ideal reconstruction of the façade as it was shortly before and after the ruinous 1117 earthquake. Moreover he examines the various changes which have given the front of the building the look of a palimpsest and he mentions the seals of the Commune: in fact Cremona used for three centuries the Cathedral's façade as its symbol in diplomatic seals.

---

1. General view of the town from St. Michael Church; 2. Largo Boccaccino; 3. Via Porta Marzia, apses of the Cathedral.

The Cathedral

According to the first plan the façade should have been enclosed by two towers and the façade of the Cathedral of Piacenza, as has been proved, should also have had two Norman towers whose construction later interrupted. The front of the Cathedral, with its saddle roof sliding down along almost unending slopes and enclosing the side apses can be seen on a Cremona seal dating back to 1250; in it, five elegant turrets crown the hip outlines and enclose a big rose-window under the cusp. The effect created by such a façade is that of a wide flat surface made lighter by single-light

3

2

mullioned windows opening in a regular arrangement on different levels. Another seal dating back to a period between 1283 and 1334 shows significant changes: the façade is more slender, it has only three turrets, a prothyrum, an open gallery and is pierced by a number of single and two-light mullioned windows which give it an aerial beauty.

For reasons connected with the size of this publication we must now go back to the narration interrupted at the time when, shortly after the

ruinous earthquake, the construction of the Cathedral was resumed. To this purpose an event and a date are constantly mentioned by all local historiographers i.e. the consecration of the Cathedral by bishop Sicardo in 1190, who, strangely enough, did not mention it in his works as he certainly should have. What is undoubted is that the Cathedral existed already in 1196 given the fact that the Baptistry had been initiated in 1167.

The charm of the Romanesque world consists not only in the mere building of churches or small Oratories but above all in the squaring of stones, the baking of bricks, in all those humble gestures expressing a dignity now disappeared and in a sense of everyday life and the Divine which shapes thoughts, imagination and the meaning and understanding of life itself.

We would like indeed to know the names of all the workers who moved and cut stones, of all those stone-cutters and bricklayers working together with carpenters and smiths with the modesty of simple craftsmen and with the same ingenuous enthusiasm they would have had on starting out for a pilgrimage to the Holy Land or to Compostela: unfortunately the Fabric's registers did not hand down their censuses to us. Even the authors, almost always anonymous, who through their different attitudes and ingenious solutions were able to produce real masterpieces of art are not appropriately remembered: they are mentioned, as is the case for Cremona, by the general name of «Master of the Months», «Master of the

Prophets», «Master of the Telamones» or in a still more generic way as «Wiligelm's workshop» or «Benedetto Antelami's workshop».

When work was resumed again a number of decorative fragments of the first temple emerged from the ruins of the partial fall of the Cremona Cathedral and they were reused in a very free way during the reconstruction. **The four main Prophets, Daniel, Ezechiel, Isaiah and Jeremiah** are closely related to the architectonic structures of the main portal, and stand frozen in an unnatural plasticism which gives them a grave and solemn air. The winding lines of their outlines, communicating a serious but already expressive sense of motion are not carved with harshness: on the contrary they create light and shade reliefs with skilful lighting effects. According to critics this «Master of the Prophets», a significant artistic figure in the Lombard Romanesque, had French models as his source of inspiration; he was influenced by the art of Southern France where a Late-Roman tradition was still alive. Clinging to the structures of the high and very splayed portal are also **telamones, symbols of the Evangelists and animals from the Apocalypse**, all figures having such compact and tight volumes as to make some famous scholars believe that they could be ascribed to the activity of Wiligelmo himself.

In order to understand the meaning of such figures with grinning faces, swollen bellies, palmated hands and prehensile feet it is necessary to go back to the Nordic culture or to read the works by Alcuino or by his pupil Rabano Mauro.

3

The people watching that almost evil vegetation and those almost monster-like figures from the church Square could not by any means understand the symbolization created by the monks' imagination, always keen on exorcizing evil spirits. The prothyrum itself, supported by two columns resting on the rumps of two lions grasping snakes and dragons had also a symbolic meaning: the Lion is the expression of the fair force triumphing over malice represented by the Snake and the Dragon. Therefore the Lion, the King of Beasts, was the symbol of Christ.

When the workers of the group of Benedetto Antelami (13th century) were replaced by those from the town of Campione, to whom the beautiful ogival prothyrum supported by **massive lions** sculptured by Gianbonino da Bissone is to be ascribed, many sculptured pieces, both from the times of Wiligelmo and from those of Antelami, were probably moved elsewhere. Some of these pieces are **the horn-player**, **the crowned King** (on the prothyrum's front), the **Virgin with Child** (to the right, above the open gallery of the prothyrum), and the **frieze of Months and Seasons** (above the ogival arch of the prothyrum).

These precious documents of the Romanesque period are once again to be ascribed to a generic «Master of the Months» who showed in his works influences coming from Benedetto Antelami. This figured calendar also told another story: the everyday's toil of humble country folks represented month by month. The Medieval world's belief in astronomy and astrology is also not to be forgotten: the succession of seasons and months is represented together with the signs of the Zodiac. Even though the figures of Cremona derive undoubtedly from the ones created by Antelami in Parma, it is easy to note a personal expressiveness and a free imagination in the resolute narration of the «Master of the Months». It almost seems that sculpture is freed from the bonds which link it to architecture in the same way as the new society of the city state was then trying to free itself from the imperial and feudal oppression.

In those Medieval days a Cathedral's façade was like a wide page and its stone rows like lines on which it was possible to write, using a chisel, the most significant events in the religious and civil history of the town. Therefore, before considering the two façades of the transept, the apse area and the Cathedral's interior, and although the works belong to different periods, let us linger for a while over the three statues which tower solemnly from the high prothyrum, the sarcopha-

Cathedral: *1. Cathedral façade; 2.-3. Central portal: prophets Jeremiah and Daniel above, Isaiah and Ezechiel below; by the sculptor Master of the prophets; 4. Prothyrum, columniferous lion sculptured by G. Biassone; 5. Madonna with Child, to the right, above the small loggia of the prothyrum.*

11

gus of Folchino Schizzi by Bonino da Campione (1327), and over the sarcophagus of Andrea Ala, sculpted in 1513 by Gaspare Pedone.

In the middle of the small open gallery, above the prothyrum, is **the Virgin with Child**; to our right, **St.Omobono** and to the left **St.Imerio**. Originally they were in niches of the counterfaçade and they were moved to the present position during the 15th century when, as will be discussed later, the Cathedral's façade underwent further changes. It has been rightly noted that there is a connection linking the religious events which occurred in Cremona in the first decades of the 14th century and the making of these three statues by a Tuscan sculptor. Ranieri del Porrina from Casole di Val d'Elsa was appointed Bishop of the town in 1296; he occupied the Bishop's seat from 1297 to 1298, but he governed the Diocese until his death in 1312, through Brother John from S.Giminiano and the notary Nicola D'Oddone from Siena. In addition, the community of Cremona, putting aside its former Ghibelline policy, had become reconciled with the «Città Nova» (new town) and, through the 1270 Statutes it allowed commercial relations, thus abolishing even the corporative monopolies. A provision from the «Gabella Magna», in 1300, decreed that «every citizen or merchant of the town or from the district of Florence is free to come and go and stay as he likes». Although the civil and religious history of this period is fairly good outlined, the name of the author of these three valuable works remains still unknown. The names of Balduccio and Gano from Siena, which have been repeatedly suggested by scholars, are not convincing enough. However they represent an aspect of that cultural atmosphere, clearly Gothic and pathetically dramatic, which Giovanni Pisano, even if taking up the classical maturity of his father Nicola, was able to fix in his works. The Madonna of the prothyrum of Cremona shows too much resemblance to the typical «Madonnas» by Giovanni Pisano rising on the spiral pedestal of the fluted mantle, to be able to represent the calm dialogue between Mother and Son. On the other hand, in the figures of the Saints Imerio and Omobono nervous torsions are appeased, the dense mantle folds become wider and the calm classical maturity seems to come back in their faces, particularly in the Saint merchant Omobono's.

The above-mentioned Masters from Campione, active in Modena as well as in Lombardy, carried out in Cremona the marble facework of the façade towards the end of the 13th century. Giacomo Porrata from Como enlarged and made more beautiful in 1274 the *big central rose-window* following the example of Nordic Cathedrals. These

numerous and very active hands worked practically everywhere over the whole 14th century, building and decorating tombs both in the old Romanesque churches and in more recent, Gothic ones, according to a new taste in an art which was then more concerned with decorating than with celebrating and had rather ornamental than structural purposes. The *sarcophagus of Folchino Schizzi*, displaced under the portico of the façade in 1890, was once inside the Cathedral on one side of the chapel devoted to St. Catherine. The elegance of forms of Bonino from Campione, which is graceful but not affected and not at all mannered, made him very appreciated and sought after, particularly for the decoration of tombs. As far as Gothic tombs are concerned, it should also be noted here that Bonino from Campione before going to Verona to build the tombs of the Della

Cathedral: 1. Prothyrum: statue of the Virgin with Child in the middle; on the visitor's right St. Omobono, on the left, St. Imerio; 2. The Virgin with Child; 3. Frieze of the months: April and May; 4. Frieze of the months: September picks grapes with a woman holding Scales; 5. Frieze of the months: July leads horses on the threshing-floor, resting on the lion's back.

1

Scala family had replaced in Lombardy the Pisan sculptor Giovanni di Balduccio, who, as already mentioned, is seen by some scholars as the author of the Virgin and of the Saints Omobono and Imerio. As for St.Augustine Church we will only examine two panels coming most probably from another funeral monument sculptured by the Master from Campione but later on divided up.

On the other side, beside the right lateral door, is the *sarcophagus of Andrea Ala*, which has been there since 1892 but was originally embedded in a wall near the St.Michael altar inside the Cathedral. The varied activities of Gaspare Pedone, born in Lugano and arrived in Cremona in 1499 to build capitals and the fireplace (now in the Municipal Palace) in Raimondi Palace and the Trecchi mausoleum in St.Agatha — which will be discussed below — belong to that atmosphere of refined culture and intense building activity that the Po-valley town was then living under the Sforza family. The floral and plant decorations, elegantly outlined and delicately modelled for the Ala sarcophagus of 1513, recall the same extreme refinement of the Trecchi Mausoleum (1502-1505).

Before examining the two fronts of the North and South transepts and going round the apses let us spend some words about the rule of the Sforza family and the great building boost fostered by the Dukes of Milan during the second half of the 15th century. It is during that golden period, in 1491, that the architect Alberto Maffiolo from Carrara gave the façade its present arrangement: he demolished the central turret, cut off the cusp and placed on it a raised storey with two niches in which Giovanni Pietro from Rho would place **the statues of the Saints Peter and Paul** and **of the martyrs Marcellinus and Peter** after the architect from Carrara had left Cremona perhaps because of quarrels with members of the Church board. The storey was in its turn crowned by a tympanum of vague classical inspiration which, in addition, was made heavier by adding a turret in the style of Bramante. The two big lateral volutes served as a connection between the pediment and the part underneath. When it became necessary (towards the end of the 16th century) to place the

emblem of Nicolò Sfondrati, who had meanwhile become Pope Gregorio XIV, in the middle of the tympanum, the volutes, the turrets and the tympanum itself were changed again by Angelo Nani (? -1611), Pietro Capra (1571-1651) and by Giovanni Francesco Divizioli.

In the meantime, between 1493 and 1497 Lorenzo de Trotti, starting from the left side of the façade close to the Torrazzo, had raised five arches in the style of Bramante to which five more arches were added in 1515 thereby replacing the modest wooden portico which connected the Torrazzo, the Cathedral and the Baptistry. Trotti was also asked to build a small open gallery over the portico which was finished in 1524, as well as five arches on the right side of the Cathedral (1548). The statues, placed over the parapet (1726) were sculptured by Giorgio Antonio Ferretti from Como in 1739.

Until now we have considered the Cathedral as having still its original basilican plan with one nave and two aisles ending in the corresponding apses. Actually its massive Romanesque structure was enlarged between the 13th and the 14th centuries by the raising of the transept and the sacred building took on therefore a Latin-cross plan. The transept's wings were completed by two beautiful façades.

Turning left we come to the small Boccaccino square until we reach via Janello Torriani, as seen from here, *the front of the north wing* rises stately. It was begun in 1261 and finished in 1288 and in 1319 it was restored after an earthquake had badly damaged its façade twenty years before. Now the façade has a typical saddle roof with a gallery along the hip lines, crowned by three polygonal turrets and divided by two slender buttresses. The aerial three-mullioned open galleries and the three big rose-windows represent the most remarkable light and shade effect which would be also repeated around 1339 in St.Augustine Church. If we follow the wide curve of the road — a dense block of houses occupied this area until 1931 — we can admire the beautiful *apses* with their slender pilaster strips, the crowns of the small arches and the fretwork in the small open galleries, divided by clear small columns. Under the columns of each arch are some mascarons which, because of their impressive and almost barbarian expressiveness have been called «the petrified». When our round trip is completed, after a few steps we come to the front of the *façade of the South wing* which, although there is disagreement among the historians, could be dated back to the middle of the 14th century. There is evidence that works were ended in 1374. The scheme of this front is the same as that of the North façade, even if it is developed with a different sensibility. Every architectonic and decorative

element in fact is kept on the surface, thus reaching the effect of a diffused luminosity and of a refined pictorialness which is the result of light lingering upon the elaborate frames of the rose-windows and of the big windows which enclose a graceful small open gallery.

Walking along the former Cemetery of the Canons we come back to the portico erected, as mentioned above, by Lorenzo de Trotti between 1548 and 1550. After entering through the right door let us go to the middle of the nave which rises in its broadness over the massive frames of the graceful pillars: these end in the slender ogival vaults which were added later on the Romanesque structure. Below, along the whole nave, is *the women's gallery* which, by partially lightening the other walls, almost restores the lost balance between this impending mass and the empty space underneath between the pillars. Above the rhythmical succession of the arches the narration cycle of the **Life of the Virgin** and of the **Life of Christ** is displayed on the whole nave's length. This work is clearly to be referred to the art of the 13th and 14th centuries and particularly to painting which played an educational role: it was like a text book for those who could not read. The whole Sacred Revelation, to which the Legend of the Virgin and the Stories of the Saints were also

added thus forming the so-called «Bible of the Poor», was translated into the universal language of painting and displayed in successive pictures, very close to each others on superimposed areas from left to right and from above to below on the white walls of churches as they were pages of a book. At the beginning of the 15th century the humanistic culture abandoned the Gothic tradition: paintings were no longer made for uneducated people but for those who were able to read and write and who knew the texts of the Revelation. The Cathedral's cycle was therefore no longer aimed at educating but was on the contrary consistent with the educated and refined ideals of the new society represented by rich merchants and lucky bankers.

The pictorial decoration — indeed one would rather call it «historyation» because it is not so much a laudatory tale as a human and divine poem about human salvation — begins on the first of the left arches with the **apparition of the Angel to St.Joachim** followed by **St.Joachim meeting St.Ann**. These events and the following two are drawn from James's protogospel, an apocryphal text of the 2nd century in which the story of Joachim and Ann, the parents of Mary, is told together with other events concerning the Virgin's childhood. On the second big arch are the **stories of Mary's birth and of her marriage to St.Joseph**, followed on the third arch by **the annunciated Virgin** and **the Visitation of Mary and Elisabeth**. Now the Life of Christ begins with the

Cathedral: 1. Portico of the façade: Folobino Schizzi's sarcophagus, sculptured by B. da Campione in 1327; 2. Northern façade of the transept; 3. The apse's side.

15

2

tales of his **Birth** and **Circumcision** which cover the fourth big arch. Boccaccio Boccaccino (c. 1466-1525) was the first artist from Cremona who was asked in 1514 to fresco the beginning of this poem of salvation: on 12 April of that year he received 100 imperial lire on account of the agreed 1000 lire for the first two frescoes, dated 1514 and 1515 respectively. Judging by this cycle some have rightly spoken of a previous journey of Boccaccino to Rome; he seemed in fact to be more attracted by the classical sweetness of Raphael than by the bursting titanism of Michelangelo. The gentle grace of Raphael not only awoke in the elder Lombard painter the dreaming atmospheres by Perugino who in 1494 had painted the Roncadelli altar-piece, now preserved in St.Augustine Church, but also rekindled the throbbing, light colours by Giorgione. In Boccaccino's figures all notes of humanity are gently struck, thereby reaching the highest lyricism of the whole Cremonese painting hereafter; from the tender and chaste warm-heartedness of old age between St.Ann and St.Joachim to the conscious certainty of the Virgin of the Annunciation; from the virginal trepidation of the

betrothed to the motherly apprehension of the Nativity.

The Adoration of the Magi and **the Presentation to the Temple** follow on the fifth arch frescoed in 1515 by Gian Francesco Bembo from Cremona. The painter's signature on a marble fragment of the first fresco is significant: it reads «BEMBUS INCIPIENS», which means «the beginning Bembo». As a matter of fact this is the first documented work by this young painter who, together with Altobello Melone, almost of his same age, became the predecessor of that Cremona opposition painting, that is to say anticlassical painting, which loved the expressive Nordic harshness.

The monumental organ sound-box which interrupts the narrative cycle was first commissioned to a carver, Filippo Vianini, who worked following a plan by the painter Giulio Campi (c.1505-1573). In 1542 the «marengone» (a dialect form for carver) received the first account of the payment for the sound-box, but he died two years later thus forcing the members of the Church Council to order, on that very year, the continuation of the work by another carver, Giuseppe Sacca who probably asked Campi through the Fabric's Prefects to draw up a new plan.

1. General view of the monuments; 2. Cathedral's interior.

although he had proved his good qualities in the previous evangelical episodes, was asked by members of the Church Council to paint works having «more beauty than the work painted for Master Bochacino». He completed five panels starting with the **Last Supper**, ended in 1518 - and not, as is always reported, in 1517. This first fresco is particularly interesting because it accounts for the rapid spreading of the most famous work by Leonardo in Lombardy. To tell the truth the fresco by Altobello Melone had a precedent in Cremona i.e. a painting by Tommaso Aleni, also called Fadino (1500-1515 doc.) finished in 1508 for the refectory of the Monks of St.Sigismund. In spite of the supreme beauty and the remarkable stylistic unity of the original by Leonardo, the work by this eccentric painter from Cremona is clearly anticlassical: in it every balance of form and composition is broken by a nervous and tormented hand. The following scenes are also by Antonello Melone: **the Washing of the feet** and **the Agony on the Mount of Olives**; then **the Arrest of Jesus** and **Jesus before Caiaphas and the Judges of the Law**.

The following scenes from Christ's Passion were differently interpreted by Gerolamo Romano, also called Romanino (c.1486-1566), who came to Cremona in 1519 after being asked to paint two of the arches. The impetuous and quarrelsome painter from Brescia represented **Jesus before Pilate**, **the Flagellation**, **the Thorncrowning** and the **Ecce Homo** in pictures full of flashing colours. His excited imagination was still

Beyond the sound-box Altobello Melone (1480/85-c.1539) frescoed **the Flight to Egypt** and **the Slaughter of the Innocents** adding the painting date: 1517. The green restlessness of Gian Francesco Bembo seems more nervously strong in the works by Melone because of a convulsive motion animating his scenes and of a nervous vibration of light on characters and backgrounds. This first part of the sacred «history» was ended in 1518 by Boccaccio Boccaccino with his fresco **the Dispute of Jesus among the Doctors in the Temple**. The Roman influences from the School of Athens by Raphael are clearly recognizable in the wide architectonic setting of the scene, in the grave expressions of the Doctors, as if they had been taken by surprise, although in a carefully studied posture. On the opposite side the cycle was continued by Antonello Melone who,

Cathedral: *1. St. Gioacchino meets with St. Anna; 2. Virgin Mary's birth; 3. Mary's visitation to Elisabeth, works by Boccaccio Boccaccino; 4. The Crucifixion (1521), a fresco by A. De Sacchis (1483-1539) called Pordenone.*

more animated by the Nordic models of Altobello thereby giving colours an unusual luministic glimmer enhanced by a rapid and nimble brush work. Romanino should also have painted the end of the narration cycle on the three remaining spans if quarrels between him and the Fabric Prefects had not induced them to assign the work, in 1520, to Giovanni Antonio de Sacchis, also called Pordenone (1483/4-1539), who in the ledgers is mentioned as «pictor modernus» (modern painter). Also a restless personality, Pordenone was always in search of effects of dramatic grandiosity often to the detriment of poetry. First of all he ignored the division into two parts of the space above the spans, a rule which had almost always been followed by his predecessors; he chose on the contrary a continuous broad scene as can be seen in **the Ascent to Calvary**, the **Meeting of Veronica** and in the **episode of Jesus nailed to the cross**. The quiet and almost classical paintings by Boccaccino, the restless sensibility of Bembo and Altobello and the fluid and passionate inspiration of Romanino all seem archaic thoughts if compared to the tumultuous representations by Pordenone. The impetuous **Crucifixion**, frescoed by the painter from Friuli on the large counterfaçade wall and enclosed in 1641 by a golden frame, a work by Carlo Natali (1586-1683), is animated by the most entangled scenes, the most daring foreshortenings and the most declamatory attitudes carried out by a ceaseless burning temperament.

Below this big fresco, on the right side of the entrance door, Pordenone painted a compact and mournful **Deposition**. A quite recent restoration carried out in 1987 revealed in all its splendour the unexpected preciousness of a luminous colouring which, far from spoiling it, enhances the strong plasticism hardly noticeable in the dull frescoes examined above.

On the left side Bernardino Gatti, also called Soiaro (c.1495-1576) painted in 1529 a **Resurrection of Christ**. This artist from Cremona although drawing inspiration from the over-emphatic representations by Pordenone also reveals the Roman mannerism which had been brought to Mantua by the painter Giulio Romano (1492-1546), a loyal collaborator of Raphael in the Vatican Rooms, and by Baldassarre Castiglione.

Let us now look again at the nave to examine **the Redeemer among the Saints Omobono and Peter the exorcist, Imerio and Marcellinus** fres-

19

coed by Boccaccio Boccaccino in 1506. Although it is the last painting in the strict representation of events it was painted before all the other frescoes of the cycle. As a matter of fact the represented texts, whose succession was decided by the Fabric Prefects, were not arranged haphazardly: they have a beginning and an end. If on the one hand the Redeemer, enclosed by a blazing Gothic mandorla, may recall the archaic image of the «Pantocrator» (the Almighty) standing out in golden apses, it represented on the other the starting point of a particular doctrinal plan: the glorification of Christ and of the Virgin, to whom the Cathedral is devoted. Frescoes were therefore painted as they were conceived in the mind of the artists. This is why thirty **busts of figures from the Old Testament**, among whom are some Prophets, were painted in 1573 inside medallions by Vincenzo Campi (c.1525/30-1591) and his pupils Cristoforo Magnani (1545-c.1585), Francesco Somenzo and Cristoforo Agosta (1570-doc.1597) on the triangular area enclosed by the arch and

Cathedral: *1. The Deposition of Christ, a fresco by Pordenone (1522); 2. The Resurrection, a fresco by Bernardino Gatti (1529); 3. Altar-piece and apse with the Saviour between the Saints Omobono and Peter the exorcist, Imerio and Marcellinus, frescoed by Boccaccio Boccaccino (1506).*

the false impending frame. Such a highly conceptual lesson, which only few people in Cremona could understand in its deepest meaning, would be repeated by Campi and his pupils in the 16th century in the Churches of St.Sigismund and of the Saints Margherita and Pelagia, as we will discuss further.

Let us now start our visit from the right aisle thereby informing the reader that the present publication will obviously not examine all the works preserved in the Cathedral but only some of them.

The **altar**, devoted **to the Saints Catherine and Donnino** (the first to the right) was erected and dated by Giacomo Schizzi in 1357. By order of St.Carlo Borromeo, who came to the Cathedral in 1575 as Apostolic Visitor, this altar was also given the «title» of another one, an altar which lies close to a column and is devoted to the Apostles Philip and James. In 1522 Giacomo Schizzi, Canon of the Cathedral and General Vicar of the Diocese, asked to be represented in a pious attitude on the painting **the Virgin and Child with the Saints Philip and James** by Pordenone. The spectacular marble altar-piece is a work by Giovanni Battista Natali (1630-1700), helped in the plastic decorations by Giacomo Bertesi (1643-1710) who, as reported by documents testifying the presentation and carrying out of plans from 1668 to 1669, was one of the most skilled collaborators of Natali. The following **altar devoted to St.Eusebius**, erected as a votive offering for the avoiding of the 1630 plague, had also an imposing altarpiece after 1667 when Natali became architect of

the Cathedral's Fabric.

The chapel of the Blessed Sacrament lies at the end of the nave in front of the one of St.John the Baptist, now called of St.Mary of the People, which occupies the left aisle. Archive documents reveal that, on 14 November 1569, Bernardino (1522-1591) and Giulio Campi (c.1505-1573) for the paintings, Giovanni Battista Cambi, also called Bombarda, for the stucco works and Francesco

4

Dattaro, also called Pizzafuoco, (? -1576) for architecture were commissioned the arrangement of the whole chapel according to the purest 16th century mannerism. However, on 18 June 1633 the Fabric Prefects and the Priors of the Confraternity of the Blessed Sacrament commissioned the rearrangement of vaults and lateral walls to Carlo Natali, the newly appointed Fabric's architect. Stucco workers Giovanni Battista Boffa (1601-1674) and Giovanni Angelo Galansino from Lugano worked together with Natali on that occasion. In order to obtain effects of greater brightness and majesty, members of the Church Council decided at the end of 1634 to have that stucco work and relief decoration gilded by Paolo Pesenti and Giovanni Lucio Manara. The rearrangement was ended in 1638 when works painted by the two Campi for the first arrangement of the chapel were also hanged on those walls. Two more canvases by Giovanni Angelo Borroni (1684-1772) were added in the 18th century. On the right wall of the first span, a classical frame of gilded stucco encloses on the lower part **the Emmaus Sup-**

per, a work by Borroni; on the upper one is **Melchizedek's Sacrifice** by Bernardino Campi (1569). On the opposite wall, inside an identical frame, hangs **the Apparition of the Resurrected to Magdalene**, one of the last works by Giovanni Angelo Borroni; above is **the Collection of the manna** by Giulio Campi (1569). In the following span, to the right of the altar on the Blessed Sacrament, are hanged two canvases by Bernardino Campi painted in 1569. The lower one represents **the Washing of the feet** and the upper one **Lazarus' Resurrection**. To the left of the same altar Giulio Campi painted in 1569 **the Last Supper** below the **repenting Magdalene at Christ's feet**. Outside the chapel, on the right side, there is a steep small stair leading up to the *Crypt* with one nave and two aisles and vaults supported by coupled columns from the Romanesque period. The controversies related to the arrangement of the crypt were probably caused both by the fact that the «Instructions» given by St.Charles during his Apostolic Visit to the Cathedral in 1575 were not immediately followed, and by the dismemberment of the tomb of the Saints Marcellinus and Peter which had been in the town church of St.Thomas since 1078 and was moved to the Cathedral in 1602. Antonio Campi in his «Most devout Cremona» writes that, as that church was about to fall, it had become necessary to «move the bodies of the pa-

---

Cathedral: *1. Virgin Mary with Child between St. Paul and St. Donnino, panel painted by Pordenone; 2. St. Eusebio's wooden altar with the Saint raising a child from the dead, by Alessandro Arrighi (1650); 3. Sacrament Chapel; 4. The crypt with a nave and two aisles.*

23

tron Saints to the Cathedral Church». At the beginning the rearrangement was marked by complete failure: during the works, directed by architect Francesco Laurenzi in 1606, vaults caved in so that the members of the Church Council asked architects Giuseppe Dattaro, called Pizzafuoco (1540-1619) and Giovanni Battista Maloio to replace the incompetent Laurenzi on 13 August of the same year. After being moved to the Cathedral, the urn of the two Saint Martyrs remained almost abandoned among marbles in a store-room under the sacristy of the Canons called «Cemetery Sacristy». The earliest document testifying of the real desire to reassemble the beautiful urn from the 16th century is dated from 9 January 1609. Then, for a whole year the Fabric's ledger registered payments to the stone-cutter Matteo Galetto from Brescia for some small statues which were to be put around the sarcophagus. The crypt and the three other tombs devoted to the town's Patron Saints were only finished in 1614 after the solemn transportation of the nine Holy Bodies along the streets of Cremona. After the ceremony, the Relics, inside five small cases of cypress wood, were put on five altars made of marble and not, as previously planned, of bricks and mortar. To the right-hand side when entering the crypt is the *first tomb* in which the relics

of *the Saints Archelao, Arealdo, Babila and Simpliciano* are preserved: this tomb was the last in chronolgical order. In fact in 1688 the «pica preda» (dialect form for stone-cutters) Giovanni Maria Pizzetti from Brescia and Giovanni Battista Puignago completed the work started about fifty years earlier according to a plan by Giovanni Battista Natali. At the time of the solemn replacing of the saint Relics, in 1614, those of the last tomb were temporarily put in the one of the Saints Marcellinus and Peter. *The following tomb*, a work from the 13th century, contains the relics of St.Facio. On the opposite side St.Imerio is preserved inside an *old sarcophagus* of the 12th century. Further on we see the altar on which the only urn built specially for the replacing of 1614 was put. The stone-cutter Matteo Galetto carried out, according to a plan by Francesco Bigallo also called Fontanella (? -1630) and by request of the Confraternity of St.Omobono, this sarcophagus in which the most important patron saint of the town, Omobono Tucenghi was placed.

On the crypt's high altar is the *urn of the Saints Marcellinus and Peter*, perhaps the best known work of the early 16th century in Cremona. The present urn, as we will see, is the result of many and diverse changes so that its original beauty is remarkably obscured. A new sarcophagus was

commissioned for the first time in 1480 because of a vow made during the plague, the year before: the original work however, for reasons unknown, was never begun. In 1506 it was commissioned to Benedetto Briosco who was asked to complete it within two years. In addition to the statues of the two saints he should also have sculptured, according to the detailed contract, six square slabs representing episodes from the Martyrs'life, two big rectangular panels and two Angels. Briosco could not complete the work either and in 1525 Gian Giacomo Della Porta, together with the stone-cutter Paolo Sacca from Cremona, suggested a more ambitious plan which was actually almost impossible to carry out for Cremona, then passing through a severe economic and political crisis. The work remained unfinished and was commissioned again to Lorenzo Trotti who applied himself to it with scarce enthusiasm from 1527 to 1538. In the meantime the sacred relics remained in the old urn on the high altar of St.Thomas Church. The dilapidated sacred building however was no longer suitable for the preservation of the bodies of the Saint Martyrs who, according to tradition, had courageously helped the inhabitants of Cremona during the battle of Castellone fought against the Milanese in 1213. As a result of the dismemberment of the old sarcophagus, of the following replacing into the Cathedral and of the above-mentioned controversies, the tomb of the Saints Marcellinus and Peter shows heterogeneous conception and execution. Yet, in

spite of obvious formal unbalances, it contains parts of remarkable quality, particularly those carried out by Benedetto Briosco: the statues of the two Saints, the very elegant urn, decorated with finely modelled foliage and the five panels representing scenes from the Martyrs'lives. After coming upstairs again to the right aisle and turning to the presbitery, we see on the wall dividing the chapel of the Blessed Sacrament from the nave a beautiful work by Giovanni Antonio Amadeo (1447-1522), probably carried out for the tomb of St.Imerio which, however, was never built. The Lombard sculptor, who received the payments for the work in 1481 and 1484 worked in two different periods at the *panel* representing **Bishop Imerio handing out alms**. On the relief, architecture and sculpture, line and colour were wonderfully harmonized by the artist with the help of pleasant effects of ornamentation where Gothic elements still survive before turning definitively to humanistic realism. Close to the two pillars of the nave and towards the small Senatorial square are the *pulpits* built in 1820 by Luigi Voghera who used for them eight square slabs from the tomb of the Saints Mario, Marta, Audiface and Abaco, commonly known as the tomb of the Persian Martyrs and once preserved in the chapel of the Meli family near St.Lawrence Church. We can only judge the work of this tomb by what remains of it, as it was dismembered in 1804 on a proposal by Giuseppe Picenardi and sold, the following year, to the Cathedral Fabric at the price of 180 Milanese scudos; the other parts were left there to fall into disrepair to be destroyed or sold elsewhere. A masterpiece by Amadeo was thus dismembered without even a trace left to posterity for an ideal reconstruction.

Voghera, who had used for the two baldachins

Cathedral: *1. Crypt with the ark of Saints Marcellinus and Peter, by Benedetto Briosco (1506); 2. Bishop Imerio giving alms, sculptured by G.A. Amadeo; 3. Panel of the Pulpit representing Martha lowered into the well, sculptured in 1482.*

four candelabrum columns and for the pulpits six columns coming from the 15th century tambour of the «Crucifix» Oratory near St. Dominic Church, realized in this way an arbitrary division of the eight square slabs. He placed the scenes of the **cutting of hands**, the **beheading**, the **corpses thrown to the stake** and of **Marta lowered into the well** on the left pulpit (if we look at it from the apse); and those of **the Saints before Emperor Claudius, the Martyrs with tied hands before Muscianus,** the **scourging** and the **Martyrs on burning coals** on the right one. Although the influence of the «stiacciato» (a kind of bas-relief) by Donatello is evident, «innovations» from Tuscany still had difficulties in being absorbed into the imaginative Lombard Gothic vegetation where a taste for decorations was prevailing.

Let us now look at the *high altar*, a remarkable work by the painter and scenographer Giovanni Battista Zaist (1700-1757) and observe, in the middle of the apse, an unfinished *altar-piece* by Bernardino Gatti, also called Soiaro, whose style is very far from that of the luminous and aerial Ascension which he frescoed in St.Sigismund Church in 1549 and from which this **Assumption of the Virgin** clearly draws inspiration. The grandiose altar-piece of carved and gilded wood is a work by Paolo Maltempo and Domenico Capra sen. (? -1591) who operated under the direction of architect Giovanni Battista Vianino, works superintendent in the Cathedral dismissed in 1598 from his office on a charge of «negligence». The gilding was made by Pietro Martire Pesenti, remembered by local historians as the one who in 1563 devised a complicated catafalque in the Cathedral to honour senator Paolo Ala's memory.

The circularly arranged *choir* is a wooden complex of remarkable quality having 36 seats in the lower level and 45 seats in the upper one. The choir was commissioned in 1483 to the inlayer Giovanni Maria Plàtina (1455-1500) from Mantua in spite of the polemic raised by local wood masters Tomaso Sacca senior and Pantaleone de Marchi against this choice; Plàtina, however, was confirmed for the work and was asked to keep the choir of the Basilica of St.Anthony in Padua, by Cristoforo da Lendinara, as his model. The meticulous inlay work made it necessary for the artist to collaborate with the painters Antonio della Corna and Antonio Cicognara for preparatory sketches while he was helped by architect Bernardino De Lera in perspective problems. The work lasted seven years whereas the contract had stipulated that it should be finished in six. The present choir structure and position do not correspond to the original ones any longer: it was in fact moved to the apse wall in 1540 in spite of the strong opposition of the Bishop and the Canons. On the following year a sum of money was payed to a Cristoforo from Venice for the cleaning and gilding of all seats. The tarsias by Plàtina represent undoubtedly one of the most precious and significant documents of the local 15th century art. Working on wide backgrounds and skilfully using the wood's pictorial quality he realized a great variety of themes: musical instruments, still-lives, landscapes and above all clear perspective views of 15th century Cremona. The Cathedral's façade, those of St.Agata Church and of the Church of St.Peter at the Po, and the town harbour are some of the views worth mentioning. Above the choir, on the right wall, is **the Entrance of Jesus to Jerusalem** frescoed by Bernardino Campi in 1573; among the figures appearing in the evangelical episode Campi painted some beautiful portraits of his contemporaries. On the opposite wall Antonio Campi represented **the Centurion before Christ** in 1582 setting the scene on a cobbled street which recalls the image of the streets of 16th century Cremona; even the houses seen in the background with their washing hanging out seem a realistic town view.

Let us now go to the left aisle and turn right towards the *chapel* devoted to *St.John the Baptist* where once the Blessed Relics were preserved so that documents often mention it as «the Relic chapel». In 1750 the chapel was devoted to the Madonna of the People and on that occasion Giovanni Battista Zaist realized a spectacular niche, to be reached through a covered small stair behind the altar, and placed a small altar on it over which the wooden group of **Our Lady of the Assumption** was hanged, a work of the 18th century (and not by Giacomo Bertesi as is usually reported). In 1638, when the arrangement of the chapel of the Blessed Sacrament was practically completed, the symmetrical position of the two chapels stressed even more the contrast between them and the one devoted to St.John the Baptist appeared bare and without any ornament. A

Cathedral: *1. The choir, a circularly-shaped wooden group containing 36 carved and inlaid stalls in the lower row and 45 in the upper row, a work by G.M. Platina; 2. Entrance to Jerusalem by B. Campi.*

Holy Sacrament Natali worked on architectonic structures which had been planned and spatially arranged by Francesco Dattaro, now, in that of the Baptist, although keeping to the previous chapel, he developed plans himself and obliged his collaborators to follow his artificial and baroque style. A long list of expenses for these works reports the contracts with the stone-cutters Puignago from Brescia, perhaps a relative of Giovanni Battista Puignago who built the tomb of the Saints Archelao, Arealdo, Babila and Simpliciano in 1668, and Bertolino Volta (? -1648) who had been living in the town parish of St.Leonard since 1624. At that time Giovanni Battista Boffa, mentioned in the payment notes for stucco works in the first chapel, was also living in the same parish. The comparison between the plastic decoration of the two works shows clearly enough that the second chapel's can also be attributed to Boffa; as we will see he was also the author of the decorations in the St.Ignatius chapel and in the nave of St.Marcellinus and Peter Church.

On the right wall of the first span a rich framing of gilded stucco encloses in its lower part a **Christ's Resurrection**, a work by Giovanni Battista Trotti also called Malosso (1556-1619), beside which are two small panels representing **the Saints Imerio and Omobono**, perhaps a work by Fran-

modelling was therefore necessary to restore the original architectural space balance of the interior: on 19 February 1645 the Fabric Prefects commissioned to Carlo Natali a rearrangement of the vault and the lateral walls by asking him to keep the excellent work he had carried out in the previous chapel as a model. It should be noted, however, that while in the chapel of the Blessed

Cathedral: 1. The Centurion in front of Jesus, by A. Campi; 2. The Chapel of Our Lady of the People; 3. St. Rocco's altar with canvases by Luigi Miradori called Genovesino (1645); 4. The Virgin with St. Anthony Abbot, St. Jerome and Pope Gregory XIV, by Luca Gattapane (1593).

cesco Bembo; above it is **the Baptist in the desert** by Bernardino Campi (1569). On the opposite wall, inside an identical frame, hangs **the Pentecost** by Malosso, on both sides of which are two small panels representing **the Saints Rocco and Abbondio** also attributable to Bembo; above them is **Salome with the Baptist's head** by Bernardino Campi (1569). In the following span, to the right of the altar, are two canvases by Giulio Campi painted in 1569. The lower one represents **Christ's Baptism** beside which is **the Saints Peter and Paul** perhaps by Bembo; the upper one is **the Baptist's sermon**. To the left of the same altar Bernardino and Giulio Campi painted in 1569 two canvases, namely **the Baptist's Beheading** in the middle and **the Birth of Christ's Predecessor** above. Again on both sides of the central canvas are two small panels representing the **Saints Marcellinus and Peter**. It will be noted that these eight small panels, allegedly by Gian Francesco Bembo, should have formed a polyptych which was preserved in the cloister of St.Abbondio and later dismembered.

Outside the chapel, in the left corner of this transept, are *ten episodes from the life of the Patron Saint* which the Confraternity of St.Rocco commissioned in 1646 to Luigi Miradori, also called Genovesino, who had been living in Cremona since not long before; the representations were to be placed inside the Cathedral on an altar devoted to the Saint. The first idea of this votive offering for the end of the plague is reported by two petitions written by the Confraternity to the town Magistrates during the grievous plague of 1630. In those terrible months every parish and confraternity in Cremona was invoking Saints, celebrating mass and organizing processions; it would take too long to report the dozen processions which took place between April and May from one church to another. In the cornice of the gilded altar-piece, in fact, Genovesino represented a procession of people singing psalms, winding over a very long distance and oppressed by a grey, unpromising sky.

Back in the left aisle we see, by the walls, three spectacular and majestic marble altar-pieces which were carried out according to a plan by Giovanni Battista Natali between 1667 and 1670. They were commissioned in different times by Confraternities or Guilds whose ambition aimed at adorning the altar of the Patron Saint not only for devoutness but also to leave a mark of their power. *The altar* devoted to *St.Anthony Abbot* (the first to the right), was partially rebuilt in 1670 as reported by a memorial stone at its base, although in 1594 it already had a marble front enclosing the painting of **the Virgin with Child and the Saints Anthony Abbot and Paul the Hermit**. The painter Luca Cattapane on request of his client Cesare Gadio also painted **Pope Gregory XIV from Cremo-**

3

4

na in worshipping attitude at the feet of the Virgin who is represented according to the iconography of Mary as «Salus Populi Romani». The work is dated 1596.

The following is *an altar devoted to St.Joseph*, patron saint of the Guild of Carpenters and Masons who asked Natali to build in 1668-1669 a suitable crowning for their altar. It is reported that the sculptor Giacomo Bertesi (1643-1710) was in those years among the collaborators of Giovanni Battista Natali who, in his quality as Fabric architect, was completing a number of rearrangement works in the aisles and in the altar-pieces. This would perhaps explain the first work of the twenty-seven years old artist who, in 1669, carved this wooden group of the **Holy Family** where a heartfelt devotion, far from the glacial intellectualism of a culture which was hostile to feelings in a Jansenistic way, expressed itself through accents of simple classicism. The formal instruments used by Bertesi, vibrating with high expressive tension in some cases and weaker and more repetitive in others, correspond to such a sensibility.

In the last *altar devoted to the Blessed Virgin of the Graces* (1667-1668) the close collaboration between a mature Natali and the young sculptor

Giacomo Bertesi is again very clear: the latter would also hold, from 1684 to 1687, the prestigious office of architect of the Cathedral Fabric. Light reflecting on gilded surfaces and on flowery swags gives this votive chapel the appearance of a majestic scenery. Back to the Great Square and before going on to visit the remaining monuments of the town it will be of interest to linger upon the high belltower (110 mts.), usually called *TORRAZZO*, which dominates the town together with the Cathedral: the two constructions seem invincible rulers, rising as they are over the waves of darkened roofs, so as to become the emblem of Cremona itself.

Cathedral: *1. Altar of the Holy Family, wooden sculptures by Giacomo Bertesi; 2.-3. Details of the wooden group of the Holy Family.*

The Torrazzo of Cremona

From the top of the Torrazzo, which reaches the considerable height of 112,10 metres (it's the highest brickwork bell tower in the world) your eye takes in the whole velley of the Po river, from the Alpes o the Appennines.

On your easy climbing you can go over again eight centuries of the cremonese history. The massive and charming structure, dating back to the 11th/13th centuries, is a realengineering miracle.

Crossed the gate in wrought iron, one is struck by the statue of a strange personage that dominates the small courtyard from the back-wall. It is Giovanni Baldesio (Zanèen de la bala) mythic Cremonese hero who, according to a legend, had challenged to a duel and had won no less figure than the son of the emperor (maybe Henry IV or even Frederick Barbarossa: the event goes back to the XI or XII century) freeing in that way the town of Cremona from the payment of the taxes due to the empire. In a more realistic way, the duel might have been only a friendly bowls game between the Cremonese Giovanni and an important personage of the imperial court (remember that Cremona was "ghibelline" thus faithful to the

emperor). The statue of Baldesio shabby with glazed and staring eyes seems to be rather a player in the act of throwing a bowl, than a bold warrior holding a golden ball, triumphal symbol of the redeemed taxes. Anyway, Giovanni's arm entered the legend and it is part of the town banner. When you are at about a third of the height, in

Statue of Giovanni Baldesio placed in the small courtyard of the Torrazzo.

Holy relics and fragments of the Christ cross conserved in the globe on the top of the tower.

the silence of the ancient walls, you will be attracted by the ticking of the big astronomical clock: the "heart" of the Torrazzo.

In a room you can admire the mechanism, the work of Giovanni Battista Divizioli and of his son Jhon Francis who built it in 1583. It's one of most famous work of Renaissance mechanical engineering.

The clock is completely original and daily it is wound up by hand. The mechanism makes the four bars turn on the large planisphere of the principal façade of the Torrazzo. They mark the hours, the phases of the moon, the days and the months of the years, the constellations and the signs of the zodiac. The fourth double bar is the most interesting part of the mechanism: it brings to an end its revolution every eighteen years and three month; moreover when at the same time it lays upon the sun and the moon bars it indicates the eclipses. At the 334th step, on your left you can notice a closed door: it's the door of the cell of the bells.

If you appear at the big inside mullion windows with two lights you will be able to admire seven heavy bells; each one of them is dedicated to a Saint: S. BARBARA AUROSIA (a night flat), S. ANTONIO from Padova (F), S. NICOLA da Tolentino (E flat), S. AGATA (D flat), S. TERESA (C), S. MARIA LAURETANA (B flat) and in the centre of the room, the biggest one, dedicated to the patron Saints of the town: S. OMOBONO and S. IMERIO (a low flat); this bell weighs, without the counterweights and the clapper, 35 quintals!

This last one is the most important because it accompanies the joyful and unhappy events of the community of the parish. At the end of your climbing you are on the elegant little terrace of the merlons, where a very agile spire is based. Further up there is the loggia with the hours bell.

From here everyone can admire the beautiful landscape and feel new emotions.

In the golden bowl of the Torrazzo there is a case with fragments of the Holy Cross and some others relics of Saints.

The Torrazzo is regulary open to the visitors every day from Easter to November 1st. In the remaining period it is open on Saturdays, on Sundays and Holidays.

During Christmas ti me it is open every day because of a fascinatig Crib.

A flight of stairs in the inside of the Tower and the mechanism of 16th century astronomical clock.

The Torrazzo in the moonlight. Photo by Gianfranco Soldi.

Although reported by a usually reliable historiographer like Arisi (1706), the news of an ancient belltower existing near the Cathedral already in the 8th century is not accepted as true by many, not even after recent excavations carried out in 1982 which left open a number of questions about the origins of the Torrazzo. In his Chronicle, Bishop Sicardo does not mention the big tower; it is true, however, that the bishop does not say anything about much more important events either, as we said before regarding the date of the cathedral's consecration. Therefore, the only way to draw up even an approximate chronology is to make a stylistic comparison between the Torrazzo and the massive Romanesque belltower of St.Agatha Church which, as we will see, could be dated back to the last decades of the 12th century. In order to confirm this hypothesis, some local historians have related the building of St.Agatha Church to the finding, inside that church, of a gravestone dated 1177 on which «a work» is mentioned, which was realized at the time of the agreements between Frederick «Barbarossa» and Pope Alexander III shortly after the Legnano defeat. Apart from all hypotheses there are evident formal similarities which relate these

1. The tower; 2. The crest of the city, located on the tower; 3. The «Bertazzola», or veranda, that connects the Tower with the facade of the Duomo. Above this in 1519 the ëParadise Wingí was begun; 4. The great astronomical clock that faces out over the piazza.

two buildings to one another: the main body, marked at the angles by slightly projecting buttresses and characterized by a double rib running along its whole length, together with a series of small suspended arches dividing the flat surfaces horizontally, are all elements proving the Romanesque origin of the Torrazzo. According to a document dated 1267 the first part of the big tower was practically completed by that time. Not even a decade later, so reports Campi, the building of the soaring spire, called Ghirlanda, was begun. Oblations for the building were still being collected in 1297 and works ended in 1305. While the massive structure underneath rises in the uniform warm colour of bricks, which turns red when caught by the light, the upper one, typically Gothic, emphasizes its lightness through a refined matching of bricks and white marbles.

The big *astronomical clock*, showily overlooking the Piazza, is also worth mentioning. The first clock, whose face was painted in 1483 by Paolo Scazzoli, dates back to 1480. One century later, in 1582, it was necessary to modify its whole mechanism because of the reformation of the calendar by Pope Gregory XIII (called after him

Gregorian reformation). The patient work was commissioned to Giovanni Francesco Divizioli who was helped by his father Giovanni Battista (? -1601), registered in 1576 as «feraro de chiavadure» (lock blacksmith) and living at that time at the parish of St.Leonard. Painters Giovanni Battista Dordoni and Martire Pesenti realized the dial-face: however, as Giovanni Francesco Divizioli modified the clock's functioning again in 1623, Giovanni Battista Natali painted, fifty years later, another version of the whole dial-plate. Giuseppe Natali (1654-1720), the son of Giovanni Battista — not to be mistaken for the painter as is now being done — partly changed in 1710, the dial's figures which were painted again in 1787 by Giacomo Guerrini (1718-1793) and Giovanni Battista Pagliari (1741-1816). Further renovations continued up to the first decades of the 20th century; the most recent one, carried out in 1974, was assigned to the brothers Vincenzo and Piero Ferraroni for the mechanism and to Mario Busini (1901-1974) for the paintings.

Cathedral: inside

The Baptistry

Today the octagonal massive structure of the Baptistry stands alone on the South side of Cathedral Square; in the past, however, according to the 15th century tarsia by Plàtina (1455--1500) it was connected to the Torrazzo and the Cathedral by an arcade and it was surrounded by stores. In fact, amid great confusion the brick market had its stores close to the sacred building which had been erected according to the wishes of the whole community as an emblem of religious glories and civic dignity. Models of a tile and a brick can still be seen engraved on the Baptistry's perimeter base towards St.Antonio Maria Zaccaria Square. In addition, although these are minor events in the historical evolution of the monument, but nonetheless significant given the importance ascribed to the building, in a petition sent by the town's pipers to the Cathedral Fabric in 1536 we read their request to be paid more for the music they played on Saturdays in the Baptistry. In spite of the fact that the sacred building had originally other entrances, which were later walled up, the constant bustle of the square induced the members of the Church board to open the main entrance and to cover the sides looking to the Cathedral and the square with a variegated marble decoration. The Baptistry was founded in 1167 and we also know the date when the internal flooring, the prothyrum and the elegant small open gallery, which was crowned above by a smooth brick surface having two round windows on both sides, were finished. It was then the second half of the 16th century and these restructuring works were commissioned to Gabriele Dattaro, Francesco Fino and Battista Ghidelli di Bornato, together with Sebastiano Nani (? -1587) and his son Angelo (? -1611), both «piccapreda». The clear, bare walls of the interior on which, majestically dilated, the outline of the early Gothic dome rises, correspond to the massive outside structure of the Baptistry, marked by projecting, pointed-edged buttresses and divided by slender pilaster strips on the whole wall which is interrupted at the same height by two mullioned windows. Even if the raising of the building carried out in the 16th century has made its original roof invisible from the outside it was not completely removed but only replaced by a copper one. On the graceful lantern which crowns the roof in the middle, is the bronze statue of **Archangel Gabriel holding a long processional cross** bearing, in Gothic letters, the date of 1369 and the name of

the Cremona Podestà, Guido Vimercati, and of Francesco Vimercati, member of the Cathedral Board.

The rapt solemnity of the Archangel is not in contrast with the apparent roughness of the modelling thanks to some refined parts of the drapery and the hair, so that somebody suggested that this rare piece from the 14th century may be the work of an expert bell founder. Two other rare and not much studied examples are also worth mentioning: the **two lion heads** fixed on the flaps of the internal door of the Baptistry.

In the end we mention the wooden altar-pieces of **Our Lady of Sorrows** (1697) and of **St.Biagio** (1700), patron saint of the University of the Battilana (woolbeaters) whose altar was once here. The former altar-piece is certainly a work by Giacomo Bertesi (1643-1710), while for the latter, although it shows clear features of the style of the skilled carver from Cremona, we do not think it proper to suggest his name. In fact in the work of Our Lady of the Sorrows a thick and almost wild foliage encloses the simple framework of the niche. The crowning shows two angels in the typical Bertesi style gliding over the foliage. In the altar of St.Biagio on the contrary, the evident architectonic scheme prevails over the artificial pictorialness of the intertwined leaves. The result is a contrasting architectonic effect between the spiral columns at the end of the altar-piece and the elegant vertical series of curly-haired angels bearing the Saint's niche.

1. Baptistry; 2. Baptistry: the altar of Our Lady of Sorrows (1697); 3. Baptistry: St. Biagio's altar (1700). On pages 36-37: performance with concert in Town-Hall Square.

The Town Hall

The façade of the Town Hall rises solemnly and full of memories in front of the likewise solemn Cathedral façade. If we would patiently examine the quantity of changes occurred in both buildings we could almost write the whole history of the town.

Cremona was given the title of «Commune» for the first time in 1098 when countess Mathilde from Canossa signed the investiture to «the people of the Church and of the Commune of the town of Cremona» for having conquered Fulcheria island and, consequently, the long-standing rival town of Crema. The strong rivalry between Cremona and the other towns of Lombardy and above all Milan induced Cremona to form a close alliance with the Emperor of Germany. It will be called that it was in Cremona that Conrad II proclaimed in May 1037 the «Costitutio de feudis» which the German Emperors tried repeatedly to impose on the riotous Communes and particularly over Milan, the most powerful among the Lombard Communes. In addition Cremona proved its faithfulness to Emperor Frederick «Barbarossa» during the Diet of Roncaglia in 1154; on that occasion the Emperor, helped by jurists from

Bologna, asked to be allowed the right to royal prerogatives, to coin-minting and to a legitimate jurisdiction over the Town Committees as a right belonging to the political system of the Holy Roman Empire. Having the right to mint coins, the symbols of the new post-feudal society, in fact, not only meant to usurp an imperial privilege because coins would then bear the Emperor's effigy and seal, but also to assert one's autonomy. Therefore Cremona was rewarded for its pro-imperial policy with the right to mint coins on its own. If in theory the jurists from Bologna and the Emperor were right, in practice Communes were now a fact which had to be taken into account. The question was actually decided on the battlefield and the courageous Lombard Communes settled the account, at least for the time being, by winning their first battle at Legnano in 1176. Cremona joined the Lombard League, which had most contributed to the victory, as a last town in 1167 thereby turning its back on the Emperor to whom it had formerly been allied against Crema and Milan. Hostilities, however, did not end at all as the third Suevian Emperor, Frederick II was determined to restore Imperial authority against the Pope's will and the Guelph Communes' resistance. Cremona was divided into two factions: the noble one, mostly formed by citizens

1

enriched by trade, remained Ghibelline and continued to live within the boundaries of the ancient Roman «castrum»; while the more popular faction, made up of craftsmen and merchants living, as mentioned above, in the suburbs of the «Città nova» (new town) in front of St.Agatha Church, remained Guelph. In addition to the internal struggle which was then appeased by the saint merchant Omobono Tucenghi and by Bishop Sicardo, fightings against the hated city of Milan went on: the Lombard town was defeated in Castelleone in 1213 during the battle of the Bodesine and lost on that occasion its *Carroccio* (a big, four-wheeled cart with the colours of the town, placed on the battlefield in the centre of the Communal army array) the remains of which can still be seen in the Town Museum after being preserved for a long in the Cathedral. It was in such an atmosphere that Cremona, as reported by the memorial stone walled up in the façade looking towards the square, built its Town Hall in 1206 following the example of the typical Lombard structure of the Broletto, a building which was also taken as a model by several other towns. So, the symbol of the free Commune was born, thus replacing the old «curia ducis», the Count's seat from which the name of Via Cordusio comes, a street which still exists in Milan. In Cremona the new building with an irregular plan had an ogival open gallery and wide windows which made it a real urban palace and not, as in the past, a feudal castle where citizens defended themselves. On the contrary, they gathered peacefully in the Court Hall and moved their first steps in a democratic system. A second stone, walled up in the South wall, reports of the enlargement of the Town Hall in 1245 through the building of three wings which enclosed the courtyard and the overbuilding upon the still existing Civic Tower. This beautiful example of Lombard civil architecture, with a wide Gothic arcade underneath and a first floor with pleasant three-mullioned windows, later turned into larger windows, had three entrances: the first one looking onto the square, the second one under the large tower, onto the present Cavour Square and the last one giving onto Via dei Gonfalonieri. The chronicler Jacopo Gadio reports that all the three entrance doors had bronze flaps. Moreover, the warm colour of the bricks did not prevent the halls and the portico vaults to be frescoed: in fact fresco decorations have emerged practically everywhere in recent times.

The antagonism between the two town factions headed respectively by the Town Hall and the Cit-

tanova Palace ended with the falling of Cremona under the Visconti rule, a process completed in 1334 by the formal submission of the town to Azzone Visconti. This meant the end of self-government which was marked by the transformation of the harbour into a structure used more for military than for commercial purposes. For a while Cremona seemed to be about to free itself from the domination of the Visconti seignory under the guide of Ugolino Cavalcabò, the one who had a chapel, also named after him, built in St.Augustine. But hopes did not last long. Cabrino Fondulo, who succeeded to Cavalcabò in the government of the town in 1420, sold it to Filippo Maria Visconti for 40,000 golden florins. The gradual decay of the structures of the Town Hall, also reported by documents of the Visconti and Sforza age, had become so extensive that in the second half of the 15th century a radical reconstruction was begun. The coffered wood ceiling was replaced by brickwork vaults decorated with the emblems of the town, the Visconti and the Sforza families. In addition, the large 14th century rooms took on, after being restructured, a more functional character, more suitable to the new government forms imposed by the new Seigniors. The symbols dotting the portico walls and vaults help us to understand the continuous changes in the town government.

Under Podestà Erasmo Trivulzio, in 1496, architect Bernardino De Lera transformed the three-mullioned windows of the façade into wide one-light windows in Renaissance style enclosed by the brickwork decoration of pilaster strips and replaced the Communal palace's original stone tribune with a marble one. Lorenzo de Trotti was commissioned to carry out the work in 1507 and he built it close to the central pilaster of the façade. The fall of Ludovico il Moro also caused the

---

1. The Town-Hall; 2. Loggia dei Militi (Soldiers' Loggia) and Town-Hall tower.

works to be suddenly interrupted. The St.Mark lion appeared among the emblems and was replaced by the fleur-de-lys coat of arms of Louis XII king of France when, in 1509, he came to Cremona after winning the battle of Agnadello against the Venetian Republic. After strong controversies between Francis I and Charles V, who payed an official visit to the town in 1541, Cremona came under the Spanish rule thus losing almost completely its economic prosperity. The greedy and bureaucratic Spanish government wanted the interior of the Palace to be restructured again and the work was commissioned to architect Francesco Dattaro from Cremona, also called Pizzafuoco (? -1576). Dattaro turned the Court Hall, the Room of the Decurions, the Room of the Referendary and of the Secret Council into a large gallery, a chapel and several rooms for the Chancellery, the Estate office and the office for Cadastral survey. A final rearrangement was carried out by architect Luigi Voghera who suggested to adjust the ornamental themes of the Palace to the questionable restoration taste so fashionable towards the end of the 19th century.

A majestic stair close to the door giving onto Via dei Gonfalonieri takes us to the upper floor where, through an elegant portal, we enter the Council Hall. **The Virtues of Justice and Temperance**, attributed to sculptor Giovanni Pietro from Rho, were added in the second half of the 16th century when the portal was carried out using the marble slabs taken from the 15th century single-light mullioned windows of the façade. On the background wall of the Council Hall is the plaster cast of the most beautiful portal ever built for a town palace in the 15th century. The original portal, sculptured by Giovanni Pietro and Gabriele from Rho, by Pietro from Vimercate and by Daniele Castello for the Stanga Palace, now called Stanga-Rossi St.Secondo Palace, has been in the Louvre Museum since 1875. Several pictures hang on the side walls but two of them are particularly worth mentioning: **the Miracle of the loaves** and **the Last Supper**, painted by Luigi Miradori, called Genovesino, for St.Francis Church, now demolished. The very crowded scene of the miracle of the loaves shows a witty and amusing collection of people from the Cremona of the 17th century represented in a free-and-easy and pitiless way as being ruled over by an inept Spanish government whose main features were an arrogant pride and a desolating poverty. With the same freedom from any prejudice Miradori also

4

works at the Apostles who are painted with bristly hair and beards and look as shabby and filthy as stevedores; the painter frees himself from the usual iconographical scheme by representing a grim devil chaining up Judas who impudently holds the price of his treachery. Four masterpieces of the stringed-instrument making from Cremona are preserved in a former chapel, now Hall of the Violins: the **Charles IX of France**, by Andrea Amati (1566); the **Hammerle**, by Niccolò Amati (1658); the **Cremonese ex-Joachim**, by Antonio Stradivari (1715) and **the violin by Giuseppe Guarnieri of the Jesus** (1734).

In the Council Hall is a beautiful *fireplace* signed in 1502 by Giovanni Gaspare Pedone from Lugano who mainly worked in Cremona, Lodi and Brescia. The local historian Giovanni Battista Zaist tells us how «the Noble Rulers of our town» bought this splendid piece from the Raimondi Family and placed it «in the public Palace where they used to meet in council». In addition to six beautiful capitals for the portico's columns Gaspare Pedone also sculptured for the nobleman Eliseo Raimondi two very refined fireplaces: the former is the one just mentioned and the latter is preserved by Count Trecchi in Maleo.

A statue, probably dating back to the Romanesque times, which had been previously preserved in a store-room in the Cathedral has recently been placed down the big stair beside the entrance door. According to tradition this «caryatid-figure» represents the Cremonese hero *Giovanni Baldesio*, usually known as Zanen de la Bala. Giovanni Baldesio, Gonfalonier of Cremona, allegedly challenged Henry, the Commander of the Imperial army and the son of Emperor Henry IV to a duel. The victory of the legendary Cremonese hero freed the town from the obliga-

tion to pay a high yearly tax: a golden ball which, by imperial order, had to be offered to the Count-Bishop. Behind this legendary episode lies actually a more reliable historical truth, namely the resistance of Cremona against the claims of Emperor Henry IV and the league between Cremona and nearby Piacenza, Lodi and Milan. Mathilda from Canossa herself supported the league which lasted almost twenty years.

Outside the Town Hall and down Via dei Gonfalonieri we see, on the right side of the road, one of the most beautiful buildings in the civil Lombard architecture of the 13th century: the *Soldiers' Loggia*. Built in 1292, as reported by the memorial stone walled up between the two majestic ogival arches of the façade, the Loggia was used as a meeting place for Civic guard Commanders.

In fact, the foundation stone shows the communal Gonfalon together with four lions, the symbols of the four Town Gates: Ariberta Gate, Pertusia Gate, Natali Gate and St.Lawrence Gate. This building, a symbol of communal self-government, also experienced the same events which affected the nearby Town Hall. Under the Spanish rule it became the seat of the Board of the Jurisconsults, formed by twelve jurists who as an Appellate Court adjudicated the sentences of the Tribunal. A narrow outside stair, demolished in 1871, led once to the meeting room and was wittily called «Stair of the Wolves» by the people.

1. Loggia dei Militi seen from the Bertazzola; 2. St. Jerome; 3. St. Jerome: altar dedicated to the Saint with decorations painted in fresco by G.B. Zaist; 4. St. Jerome, the dome by S. Massarotti.

St. Jerome Church

The simple structure of St.Jerome Church, once seat of the Confraternity of the Blessed Virgin of Mercy and of St.Jerome, rises on the Southern corner of Cathedral Square on the narrow Via Sicardo.

This Confraternity, which joined the Roman Arch-confraternity of St.John Decollate in 27 June 1610, was established on the initiative of some lay-men in 1436, at the time when Venturino Marni was Bishop of Cremona, in order to be of comfort to those who were condemned to death and to give them a Christian burial.

According to some local historians the brethren used to gather in different places of the town and among them in the small church of Father Ottolino Zaniboni. Three years later the Confraternity, canonically established on 28 September 1453, was given that small church as its seat, even though brethren gathered elsewhere for some time. A notarial document of 25 January 1489 proves in fact that they used to meet «in domibus sancti Mauritii» i.e. in St.Maurice's houses. In addition, in the years 1504 and 1507 Alessandro Meli was payed by the Confraternity 50 imperial «scudos» as a rent for the church. The first official approval of the statutes of the year 1459 was followed by others up to 1561. In 1599 Bishop Cesare Speciano payed the small church, also called Oratory and having a square plan and only one altar, his Pastoral Visit.

St.Jerome Church as it is today was restored and enlarged in the years from 1615 to 1624 by Francesco Capra and Rinaldo Cambiaghi who followed a plan by Giovanni Francesco Mussi. The sacred building, in which the original quadrangular plan of the Oratory was abandoned, was structured on

3

4

2

a Greek-cross plan so that two side altars devoted to *St.Jerome* and *St.John Decollate* could be added. For the building of the latter the Hospital of the Beggars, according to a notarial document of 17 July 1631, payed the Confraternity a certain amount of money on condition that an altar devoted to the Baptist be built.

The church was enlarged a second time in 1657 by architect Alessandro Capra (1608-1683) who was asked to build «the chapel of the High Altar» within one year. The architect conceived a long polygonal apse and gave the large presbitery a strong impression of depth without altering the original simplicity of the building. According to the writings of the historian Giuseppe Bresciani «the renovation of St.Jerome Church's decoration begins on 17 May 1660»; later on, this decoration will be completely covered by the 18th century

frescoes by Francesco Monti (1685-1768) who painted *the dome and the vault's medaillons* (1743); by Angelo Innocente Massarotti (1654-1723) author of *the dome's pendentives* (around 1710); by Sigismondo Francesco Boccaccino (1659-1740) (*presbitery's vault*) and by the quadraturas by Giovanni Zanardi, Giuseppe Natali (1655-1720) and Giovanni Battista Zaist (1700-1757). It is interesting to note that in 1741 Zaist was one of the members of the Confraternity together with the son of Giuseppe Natali, Lorenzo (1673-1748), also a «quadraturista» wall painter. A painted scenery giving the impression of a deeper and more variously structured space, seemingly stretching out towards distant vanishing points replaced the true rigorous architecture of St.Jerome Church. In 1666, ten years after Alessandro Capra's rebuilding, and later on in 1675 Bartolomeo Griffino carved two beautiful wooden altar-pieces for the high altar and for the altar of St.Jerome. The frescoed quadraturas in the apse and the building of a small fine balcony behind the high altar obliged the brethren to move one of the wooden altar-pieces to the altar of St.John Decollate fitting it to the picture painted in 1743 by Giacomo Guerrini (1718-1793) from Cremona.

In 1788, after the Confraternity was suppressed, this fine small church, which had been built to receive the devout brethren and the executed men's corpses, became an additional church for the Cathedral. As a result of the suppression of many parishes the statue of the Loreto Virgin was moved in 1790 from the Holy Cross Church to St.Jerome Church, thus replacing the wooden images of the Crucifix and of Our Lady of Sorrows, the last mark left by the Confraternity.

St. Imerio Church

Going down the steep paved path of Via Sicardo, past Via Plàtina, one comes into Via Aporti which goes on until the road crosses Via Realdo Colombo. There, almost confused among the houses, rises the humble façade of St.Imerio Church; as Pellegrino Merula reports, it was built on 13 July 1606 thanks to the munificence of the nobleman Cesare Vidoni, Marquess of St. John of the Holy Cross, after the approval of Bishop Cesare Speciano and the donation of two thousand «scudos» from the town. The Barefooted Carmelites, charged with the administration of the church, could start their community life in the adjoining cloister in 1608; the building, in which now only eight cells are still existing, was erected, according to Marquess Vidoni's will to allow his brother, father Giovanni Pietro of the Assumption, a man of poor health, to remain in Cremona. On 16 July 1612 Bishop Giovanni Battista Brivio solemnly devoted the church to the Saints Imerio and Teresa from Avila. In 1805, after the suppression of the Carmelites, the church became an auxiliary of St.Clement Church but was given back its title of parish on the following year when it was charged with the administration of some nearby parishes which had been in turn suppressed: St.Pantaleone Church, St.Geraldo Church, St.Erasmus Church and St.Clement Church.

The solemn and balanced arrangement of intervals among the three internal spans and the calm

3

harmony of the sacred building's proportions have always supported the hypothesis that its architect was Francesco Bigallo, also called «Fontanella», the one who is also said to have planned St.Marcellinus and St. Peter Church together with the adjoining Cloister of the Jesuits. Although this publication does not allow a thorough discussion on the chapels, we would like to draw the readers' attention to two of them, namely the first and the third one which one finds on the right hand side on entering the church. In the former, the painter Giovanni Battista Natali (1630-1700) from Cremona, a few months after coming back from Rome, painted as an altar-piece a **Madonna with Child who offers St.Anthony from Padua a lily**. It is the first work of the artist bearing a date: in fact it is to be related to a previously unknown

document reporting that on 31 May 1655 Giovanni Battista Natali acted as godfather at the baptism of Raffaele Nicola, the son of Luigi Miradori also called Genovesino, the most talented personality of the 17th century in Cremona. In 1651 the elder painter, who had been a parishioner of St.Clement for a couple of years, painted for this very church **the Rest during the Flight to Egypt** over the altar of the third chapel. The sacred theme of the work by Genovesino is deprived of its timeless sacredness and takes on a humble every-day style in which the event is depicted rather with story-telling than with celebrating intentions. Even clouds, impalpable in their atmosphere-like quality become dense▬▬▬sh bodies with unusual shapes and suppo▬▬▬▬es-tial figures with definitely human feat▬▬▬ng which are always plump children.

In the painting by Natali, on the contrary, the exuberant pictorial language of Miradori is more controlled and carried out in a lower tone as in the figure of St.Anthony who, on his knees, seems to stretch towards the Child with hands more

---

1. St. Jerome: G.B. Zaist, detail of the pilaster strip; 2. St. Imerio, first chapel on the right side: Madonna with Child giving a lily to St. Anthony of Padua, by G.B. Natali; 3. St. Imerio, third chapel on the right side: the Rest during the flight into Egypt, a detail, by Genovesino.

devout than ready to receive the chaste gift of the celestial lily. From above, the Virgin, motherly in her corporeity, hands majestically the snow-white flower to the amused Child who seems to come from the nearby picture by Miradori.

St. Mary Magdalene Church

After leaving St.Imerio Church, which stands on the corner between via Aporti and via Realdo Colombo, one turns down the latter, a street that leads to the old St.Clement Church, commonly known as St.Mary Magdalene Church. In the 19th century town topography the holy place was also given the denomination of St.Mary «in Gonzaga».

Information supplied by some local historians, according to which a temple devoted to St.Clement was already existing in the 6th century and was later turned into a parish by Bishop Crisogono, has proved unreliable. A more probable hypothesis suggests that a parish called St.Clement had existed since 1286 and that it was given the name of St.Mary Magdalene only afterwards.

In the late 16th century, after the sale of a plot of land by the members of the Vestry Board, the primitive, small church was completely rebuilt, as is reported by an inscription which has been recently discovered in the bowl-shaped vault: «M(agister) LAZARUS DE POÇAL / FECIT HANC ECCLESIAM / 1484 DIE 21 JULI». (Master Lazarus

de Poçal built this church on 21 July 1484). Perhaps on that occasion an image of Mary Magdalene was moved from All Saints' Gate to the church and this denomination became gradually more popular among the believers.

«Magister» Lazzaro Pozzali, a relative of architect Bernardino De Lera, added to the simple sloping façade, divided by two strong buttresses, a note of coquettish elegance by crowning the front with three octagonal, slender small turrets covered by a fired brick decoration attributable to Raynaldo De Stavoli, or De Stauli, who, not far from there, was running a going brick works.

The interior of the church was radically changed in 1630 by Carlo Mariani whose work has been partially brought back to its original splendour by restorations which lasted from 1964 to 1968; particularly interesting are now the flowery decoration of the vaulting cells and the series of the *Twelve Apostles* on the apse, inspired by the late Gothic style of Bonifacio Bembo.

Only two paintings have been in the church since its origins: a polyptych by Galeazzo Campi

1. St. Mary Magdalene's Church; 2. Polyptych by G. Campi and T. Aleni, also called Fadino; 3. Interior; 4. Fresco from the 15th century; 5. The Virgin attaching St. John Damascene's severed hand back, by Genovesino.

(1477-1536) and Tommaso Aleni, also called «Fadino» (doc.1500-1515) and a painting showing **the Virgin reattaching the severed hand to St.John Damascene**, a work dated 1648 by Luigi Miradori, also called Genovesino.

The polyptych, realized by the two painters from Cremona, shows the influence of Boccaccio Boccaccino (1466?-1525) and presents some typical characteristics of Perugino which are however interpreted by means of an archaizing

5

simplicity which takes into account the innovations of the Venetian painters.

In the painting by Genovesino a vivid light marks the close dialogue of the characters whose hands are intertwined and merging with the Child's pinky flesh; the heavy mantle of the Damascene, partly shadowed, continues on to a snow-white cloud which becomes a note of shrill colour over the background architecture, enlightened by a grazing light.

Church of the Holy Trinity

After visiting St.Mary Magdalene Church we go up via XI Febbraio again, passing close to the Cathedral's apses, beautiful in their lively motion, until we cross via Plàtina and then turn down via XX Settembre. The straight series of houses on the roadside guide our eyes to stop immediately in front of the simple façade of St.Gregory Church: the building interrupts the regular outline formed by the houses'shape so that its sideway position makes the road turn at a right-hand angle.

The original denomination of St.Gregory, a priest and a martyr from Spoleto, which is now almost forgotten, has been replaced by the more recent dedication to the Holy Trinity and today the church is commonly known by this name. The old dedication is due to the fact that the head and parts of the body of the Saint Martyr have been preserved in the holy place since 1369, after being moved from Spoleto to Cremona in 993 and not, as reported by the usually careful chronicler Pellegrino Merula, in 970 by Bishop Olderico. The chronicler himself, writing in 1627, also

added that the temple in which the saint relics had been preserved originally was then still unknown.

A number of documents dating back to the 12th century seem to confirm that they were at first kept in a chapel or a small church close to the Cathedral. It is therefore not surprising that another sacred building devoted to the Martyr was erected afterwards near the parish Church of St.Michael Vetere. Giovanni Maria Cassiani, parish priest in this church from 1624 to 1651, mentioned a parchment dated 26 September 1130 while drawing up a scrupulous inventory of the «writings belonging to the parish» of St.Michael during the Pastoral Visit of Cardinal Pietro Campori, Bishop of Cremona. A local historian wrote in 1926 that he had found the parchment «by chance» with other precious documents. At present the archives of this parish do not unfortunately contain anything about the long series of items mentioned by Cassiani in his inventory, but in the said parchment was mentioned the fact that Bishop Oberto had donated to St.Gregory Church all that he possessed of a certain St.Martin Church, called «de Casapagana» («Pagan-house» Church). This is probably one of the episodes along a series of conflicts between the Bishop of Cremona and the Cathedral's Canons, which had to be appeased even by the personal intervention of Pope Callisto II (1124) and later on by Pope Innocent III (1139). Questions had risen about some rights and privileges claimed by both parties as regards St.Michael Church which, in 1139, was given back to the Canons who were also allowed to appoint altar-boys for ceremonies. Twenty years had just elapsed since Pope Innocent II decided in the Cathedral's choir on 24 December 1159, with the approval of Bishop Oberto, that rights should be mutually transferred from the Capitular Canons to the priests of St.Gregory Church: the Canons gave up all their privileges in St.Michael, and the priests of St.Gregory granted them «the place where the body of the Saint Martyr lay». As the document does not specify what the expression «the place where the body lay» means, we can only suppose that it was about the patronage right to which those who looked after the tomb and the altar of the Saint were entitled. Perhaps, as a result of that, Bishop Oberto moved the head and parts of the body of the Martyr to St.Michael Church — also called St.Michael in Borgo (in the suburb) or, as is reported by that particular document and by many others as well, «St.Michael Suburb» — in 1160, according to Merula's writings.

This solemn replacing of the revered Relics of the priest and martyr from Spoleto marked the beginning of the events which eventually led to the building of the present St.Gregory Church, also called Church of the Holy Trinity. However, even before 1162, when Bishop Oberto confirmed that the body of St.Gregory should be preserved and adored in St.Michael and proclaimed that the estate of the two churches should be put together and the churches themselves considered as one, another precious document, artistically decorated although not written on parchment, proved that the Confraternity, called «St.Michael's Charity» had a reliquary made in 1148 to preserve the Saint's head. Although this reliquary does not exist any more, a trace of it has remained in the form of a writing engraved on another reliquary preserved in the Church of the Holy Trinity and dated 1480 by «magister Luchinus de Albeziis». The original inscription: «Caput Sancti Gregorii Ma/rtiris et Caritas Sancti Michaelii/ 1148 die 9 Octubris» is translated as: «The head of Martyr St.Gregory and St.Michael's Charity/ 9 October 1148». The desire to possess relics, no matter whether authentic or false ones, and the craving to see them and kiss them was so intense that churches boasted an indefinite number of such sacred objects, believers went on long and exhausting pilgrimages, and Confraternities fostered the realization of precious reliquaries and the building of altars or chapels. Perhaps, at the time of the transfer of the revered mortal remains of the Saint Martyr to St.Michael Church, the chapel or the small church near the Cathedral did not exist any more because of reconstruction works carried out after the ruinous earthquake of 1117, as previously mentioned. What is certain is that at the beginning of the 14th century only the memory of that first holy place of worship remained in the above mentioned documents and parchments. The congregation of St.Michael, however, by preserving the head of St.Gregory in the first reliquary, perhaps in the old crypt, felt in a sense obliged to hand down to the future members of their parish the memory of the first church devoted to the Saint ever built in Cremona. Therefore, in 1369, so Merula and other local historians believe, the inhabitants of the suburb of St.Michael built a small church devoted to St.Gregory. In the same year Bishop Pietro Capello, from the nearby St.Michael, transferred the head and parts of the body of St.Gregory in the specially constructed built building. It has rightly been observed that the architectonic features of the late Lombard Gothic style can be easily recognized on the right side of the church, in the one-cusp façade. Although welcoming the structural dynamics of the Gothic style, this suburban church, protected to the West by the ancient apsidal building of St.Lawrence and to the East by

2

1. Church of the Holy Trinity; 2. The Holy Trinity adored by the Saints Gregory and Filippo Neri, canvas by G.G. Fochezer.

St.Michael Fort, which Bernabò Visconti had to enlarged in 1369, chose to remain true to a balance of space which still gives it, after the restructuring works of the 16th-18th centuries, a gentle bareness, typical of the Franciscan spirit.

Now the church has only one nave with a particularly rich structure in the apse. Judging from the number of frescoes partially appearing under the surface of a thick brickwork structure which was added to the old one at the end of the 16th century, the presbitery was originally communicating with two chapels on both sides. In the late 16th century it was also decided to substitute a barrel vault, subdivided by sharp transverse arches — which, by joining the half-pillars of the nave, approximately mark the original location of the altars — for cross vaults. So it seems that the small church had a «tau»-shaped plan in which neither radiating chapels nor chapels on its sides were allowed: three chapels were simply lined up one after the other, the central one being slightly more developed and deeper. A number of interesting remains of 14th century frescoes are preserved, even if a little faded, inside the two chapels on both sides of the presbitery — the left one is now used as a belfry — but also behind the altars and the corresponding altar-pieces.

A document dated 1387, less than twenty years after the solemn transfer of the revered Relics,

51

reports that two altars devoted to St.Peter and St.Michael were then built in St.Gregory Church. The parish church of St.Michael, which could boast to have being the first Cremonese church to preserve the body of the martyr from Spoleto after the Cathedral, performed therefore, from the very beginning, a protective function for the small sacred building at its side. This particular role of St.Michael was confirmed in 1495 in a Bull by Pope Alexander VI. The bull stipulated that «the church of St.Gregory be perpetually joined and incorporated into the parish church of St.Michael»; in addition, indulgences were granted to those who had lavished funds for the church's restoration.

Finally, another event, decisive for the future of the old place of worship, is worth mentioning.

The notary Giovanni Battista Sfondrati drew up and countersigned in 1591 a detailed agreement between Giovanni Antonio Onorati, parish priest at St.Michael, and the Priors of the Confraternity of the Holy Trinity — which had been in the parish since 1336 — who were entrusted with St.Gregory Church. On that occasion the new denomination was added, which was destined to last more than the original but not less glorious one. The above-mentioned architectural changes were followed by replacements of altars and their corresponding dedications. The report of Cesare Speciano's Episcopal Visit on 2 September 1599 gives us an idea of what the church looked like eight years after the assignment. The last altar to the left was devoted to St.Christopher, while now it is devoted to Christ Resurrected (1740); it was

followed by the altar of St.Ursula, now devoted to St.Gregory, erected and decorated by Giovanni Antonio de Schizzi in 1437 and having **the Adoration of the Magi** as its altar-piece, a work by Sigismondo Francesco Boccaccino (1659-1740); the last one, devoted to St.Francis, on which the Visconti family was entitled to have the patronage rights, still has a painting by Stefano Lambri (1624) representing **the Deposition**. On the other side there was the altar of the Blessed Virgin, under the patronage of the Main Hospital but devoted, since the 17th century, to St.Carlo Borromeo. The altar-piece shows in fact **Our Lady with Child and the Saints Filippo Neri and Carlo Borromeo.** Then, where once the Annunciation altar was, is now an imposing carved and gilded altar-piece which encloses a valuable wooden **Pietà**; finally, the altar of St.Mary, now devoted to the Immaculate according to the will of Francesco Maria Farina who, in 1722, had it built at his expense.

In the first half of the 18th century the interior took on a more frivolous look because of the pleasant stucco works decorating the vaults of the spans and the capitals, and which frame two valuable paintings: the former, hanging over the entrance door, represents **the Eternal reproaching Adam and Eve after the original sin**, a work by Sigismondo Francesco Boccaccino; the latter, in the apse, represents **the Holy Trinity adored by the Saints Gregory and Filippo Neri**, a work by Giovanni Giorgio Fochezer, as he himself used to sign: this was actually the exact spelling of his name, contrarily to what is mentioned in the canonical books of the town parishes of St.Luke and St.Helena in which several different versions of his name are given. Most editors of guide-books or local art reviews have never paid to this work the attention it deserves and have systematically

mentioned a wrong date: 1703 or 1713. Actually the painting is clearly dated and signed: «JO.GEORGIUS FOCHEZER GERMANUS/ INVENIT ET PINXIT. AD: MDCCLXXIII» (Invented and painted by Jo.Georgius Fochezer Germanus, A.D. 1773). Only some events of the life of this artist from Bavaria, born in Kisselg near Lindau, are known: he worked in Cremona and Bologna where he was registered at the Clementine School of fine arts. Moreover, his permanence in Italy seems now to be documented from 1743 to 1773 and not only until 1760 in Cremona, as claimed by some scholars, when he painted the altar-piece of the Holy Trinity church. According to the book of the children baptized in St.Helena, the artist actually lived in this parish, because his daughter Paola Antonia Maria was baptized in January 1758, his son Giovanni Giorgio Emmanuele in May 1759 and his second son, born in November 1760 by Elisabetta Caterina Scanacapra, was given a «nomen italicae» i.e. a name which in Italian sounds like: Santo, Amato, Benvenuto. Giovanni Giorgio Emmanuele lived in Cremona at the parish of St.Luke until 1804.

The painting of the **Holy Trinity worshipped by the Saints Gregory and Filippo Neri** is a rather typical example of the style of this artist from Bavaria who painted his figures with rapid strokes, saturating the atmosphere with a liquid chromatism which reminds us of Borroni and, in certain respects, Bencovich.

Were it not for a confirmation of an event reported by the historian Giuseppe Bresciani — too often unfairly criticized for being unreliable — about the works of a certain Tomaso Tezano, a sculptor who worked together with Girolamo Bonetto, there could hardly have been a reason to recall that Tezano realized and signed a bell for the Church of the Holy Trinity in 1512. Another bell, found by chance at an antiquarian's, dated 1582 and bearing the signature of: «Brandimarte Faletto from Cremona», will be added in a short while on the graceful bell-tower.

Church of the Holy Trinity: *frescoes from the 15th century.*

Church of St. Michael Vetere

Today the beautiful church of St.Michael, proud of its more than millenary history and isolated in a silence which seems almost beyond reach, is all that remains of the ancient St.Michael Suburb, as it was nostalgically called by Carlo Bellò in an autobiographical booklet — and indeed this denomination dates back to the 12th century and is proved by documents.

The «twin» church of St.Lawrence, solitary in its present state of disrepair, was erected shortly before the year 1000 along via Cesare Speciano on two previous sacred buildings devoted to St.Lawrence and St.Mary. Since its foundation the church had also been devoted to the Apostles Philip and James. The year 986, during which the present St.Lawrence Church was reconstructed according to Bishop Olderico's will, represents a point of reference in the events which also affected the nearby St.Michael Church. Although documents do not say much about the foundation of the two sacred buildings which stood there before the present one, now devoted to the deacon and martyr Lawrence, we can suppose that they have existed since the 6th-7th century.

As for their position to the town it is worth

mentioning that outside the Medieval Porta Ognissanti (All Saints' Gate) (at the intersection of via Oberto Pallavicino and Matteotti avenue), and not far from St.Lawrence, a Christian cemetery was built on a pagan one. Although they are close enough to the original town centre which lay inside the ancient Roman «castrum», the traces left by the early Christian faith outside the walls prove how Christianity could germinate better outside than inside the small Roman camp. Moreover, even if the fact that a sacred building devoted to St.Agatha from Siracusa had existed since the 6th century at the other end of the town — on the place where the St.Agatha Church was built in 1077 — could not be proved, the fact is that the primitive boundaries of the old quadrangular Roman camp were changed in the early Middle Ages by the addition of two small suburbs: one to the North and another to the East. And it was on this eastern area of town, along the layout of the Postumia way which connected Genua to Aquileia, that new settlements rose more rapidly than elsewhere. The road was in fact the obligatory way for anyone going in and out of the town and it was therefore a natural consequence that, at the beginning of the Christian age, the inhabitants of the small group of houses that would later become the Suburb of St.Michael put down roots in this area. Most of them were poor people who had not find a place to live in the centre of town and looked for an abode outside the walls, where the countryside began. It was a very small settlement having no importance in the documents of those days, but it was destined to grow larger after repeated Barbarian invasions had almost wiped out the traces of the Roman civilization, as the Po river does when, after the flood, leaves on the fertile fields a layer of muddy sand which covers everything without destroying it in depth.

So, very close to the town, the small churches of St.Lawrence and St.Mary and the Apostles Philip and James rose in that order: to the historical reasons justifying their location safety reasons are also to be added. In fact those small suburban

St. Michael Vetere's Church.

settlements, later called «borghi» (suburbs) were mostly formed by precarious buildings erected at the risk of their inhabitants, for outside the town gates, undefended and unguarded, they were exposed to the dangers of robberies and raids. In case of war they had to be completely demolished and set ablaze by the inhabitants themselves who had to return inside the walls which lay close by as a perennial symbol of defence. It is therefore out of the question that a sacred building devoted to St.Michael had already existed in the 6th-7th century on the same place where it now stands, although the place itself was near a marshy ground which alone could represent a natural defence for it was only a few hundred metres from the town walls also. However, if the church existed in the troubled early Middle Ages, it was undoubtedly appeared too undefended. The Longobards, who had laid siege to Cremona for many years, finally conquered and destroyed it in 603, under their King Agilulfo in 603. Around that first church, devoted to the great warrior Saint always with his sword in hand, whom the Longobards adored far more than any other Martyr or Confessor of the faith, was most probably clustered that first small settlement, which could not yet be considered a suburb. We do not so far possess documents proving to the contrary and, to tell the truth, it seems that the dedication to the leader of the angelic host corresponds to a time immediately following the conquest of Cremona by the Longobards.

In a relatively more recent time than the one we are talking about, the almost complete lack of verifiable sources was replaced by a pseudo-historical fact suggesting the name of Queen Theodelinda who, after the death of her husband Agilulfo (615), allegedly refounded some churches of the town, including St.Michael Church. This fantastic historical interpretation, like any other legend, hides a deeper meaning. At the time of meek King Liutprand the town was rebuilt, received new inhabitants and reached a certain degree of affluence. And yet, in spite of this relatively calm period, documents continue not to mention the subject we are now dealing with, except for the «Constitution of the salt tax in the ports of the Po river» (715-730), in which the resumption of commercial activities on the river is only vaguely mentioned. At any rate we believe that that was the most suitable time for the construction of St.Michael Church which, by looking on to the countryside, encouraged the people to go outside the town walls and to trust more the protection of the bell-tower than that of the Barbarian Guardingo.

One of the questions which will always remain unanswered is about the size of the original church devoted to St.Michael. Certainly it must have been very small, so that it could be argued that it corresponded to the present crypt. Some local scholars have recently suggested this charming hypothesis but have made a mistake in dating the whole building back to the 7th century on the basis of two columns of cipolin marble, which are undoubtedly of Longobard age, and of five capitals, also datable from the 7th century. However, neither the crypt's wall structure, made of big bricks on thick lime layers, nor the indivisible unity of the external apsidal group allow a confirmation of the hypothesis. In addition to the uncertainty about the old building's size, its dating also represents an unresolved problem, even if the most probable date should not be very far from the 7th-8th century.

In his report drawn up in 1624 on the Pastoral Visit of Cardinal Pietro Campori, Bishop of Cremona, to the parish church of St.Michael, the parish priest Giovanni Maria Cassiani mentioned in chronological order a whole series of parchments and notarial documents «concerning» the church. As we said before nothing remains of all this material, which would have been really invaluable for the reconstruction of the historical events regarding St.Michael's. The first date reported on that long list was 1187, when Pope Gregory VIII assigned «perpetually» St.Michael Church with all its properties to the Bishop of Cremona. The most important and reliable date, however, for the reconstruction of a chronological order on the erection of the first building devoted to the leader of the angelic hosts is the year 1007. Bishop Landolfo confirmed to archpresbyter Benedetto his appointment of two priests who had the task to assure suitable liturgical ceremonies and, above all, to look after the church: «quoniam vetustate consumebatur» («As it was consumed by time and old age»). This simple expression represents a confirmation of the dating of St.Michael's foundation which, as is also reported by Count-Bishop Landolfo, was laid probably between the 7th and the 8th centuries. The fact then, that the building was already crumbling around the year 1000 and that its «antiquity» had irreparably peaced its mark on it, makes this dating still more probable, as it would be consistent with the date suggested for the preexisting churches of St.Lawrence and of St.Mary and the Apostles Philip and James.

Astegiano, relying on the analysis of the documents of those days, spoke of an intense building activity and mentioned a long and meaningful list: S.Luke (1035); St.Peter on the Po (1064); St.Thomas (1066); St.Gabriel (1076); St.Agatha (1077); St.John the Evangelist (1079); St.Vitalis (1088) and St.Salvatore (earlier than 1090). To tell the truth, St.Michael Church is not even mentioned, but two almost contemporary documents reveal some information of historical interest. St.Michael was mentioned in 1075 as being «outside the town of Cremona» and in 1078, «in braida», which means «on arable land» and therefore no more on a deserted and marshy area. Astegiano further recalls that the «twin» church of St.Lawrence was outside the walls in 1021, while it was within the town boundaries in 1040 and 1081. The gradual expansion of the town, which developed on both sides of the main roads leading in and out of town, explains how the new church devoted to St.Michael was erected among those small houses, on the place where the crumbling sacred building mentioned by Landolfo had stood. The homonymous «Borgo», mentioned for the first time in 1128, must certainly have had a relatively remarkable size and the parish must have been well organized. In fact the Confraternity called «St.Michael's Charity» commissioned in 1148 a reliquary for the head of St.Gregory which is still preserved in the Cathedral. Then, between 1007 and 1100, a new sacred building in Romanesque style rose on the remains of the previous one while keeping its original denomination.

As readers will remember, when we spoke of the charming but improbable hypothesis according to which the present crypt could correspond to the first church devoted to the warrior Archangel we said that the apse's structure is so homogeneous that it is not possible to distinguish or separate the two buildings erected in different times. Were it not so, we would have to admit that what had remained of the ancient place of worship, now a crypt, had determined the size of the Romanesque church. On the contrary, it is believed that the new temple was planned on purpose in its broad basilican arrangement with a nave and two aisles, more suitable for the gathering of a large congregation, with well-marked apses and with a crypt, built specially for the new church, for which only the Longobard columns and capitals, previously belonging to the original sacred building devoted to St.Michael, were used.

The intense building activity after the year 1000 shows us several groups of stone-cutters skilfully erecting clustered pillars from which capitals with intertwined foliage and beast-like figures emerged; courageously building massive arches with marked ribs; arching cross-vaults with overimposed architectural elements, full of solemn motion and commanding plastic effects. The Romanesque church was born: the expression of a society which was no longer a feudal, but a lay one and which would become a communal one. The distinction between presbyters and laymen, monks and farmers, intellectuals and craftsmen however, was still deeply rooted. Likewise in Romanesque churches, an altitudinal differentiation was added to a longitudinal distinction. In the choir, behind the altar, were those who had chosen to serve God; in the nave, the mass of farmers and craftsmen. The apsidal area was higher than the nave's floor because of the underground

crypt, and the space of the church was therefore divided up in two parts at two different levels: the presbitery's higher one, and the lower one in front of the crypt. The congregation had to remain under the presbytery and before the transept, if the church had one. No place in the church seemed more apt to preserve the Martyrs' Relics than the crypt, and the practice of building this type of underground church became then widespread. It was connected to the aisles by stairs and its space was occupied by many columns supporting the presbytery.

St.Michael Church in Cremona was also built according to that Romanesque scheme, and when Bishop Oberto transferred the head and parts of the body of St.Gregory from the Cathedral to the Church of St.Michael in Borgo, in 1160, the relics were most probably placed in the crypt, a suitable place for the silence of deep prayer and meditation. In a recent and documented study about St.Lawrence Church (1987) the different structures of crypts built in the early Middle Ages (9th century-early 11th century) are analyzed and particularly the «oratory»-crypts with their small, irregular spans covered by cross-vaults on transverse arches; the study underlines the fact that this architectonic scheme did not spread in Italy before the year 1000.

The aim of the present guide-book, clearly a popularizing work, leads us to begin our visit with the apsidal area which perhaps was less affected by the ravages of time than by man's, The survived central apse stands out distinctly from the church's main body and is dotted by a series of long corbels in which the depth of the spans diminishes gradually, according to the usual scheme of castles' fortified towers. These small blind arcades have a linear and decorative value which lightens and makes more precious the swollen volume of the apse, looking even more marked and turgid for the absence of the two minor apses which should have represented a balancing element. A note written in 1926 by the parish priest Giovanni Varischi about the several restoration works carried out in St.Michael between the 19th and the 20th centuries, reveals that in 1844 the building of a new bell-tower, more imposing than the previous one, caused the left apsidiole to be demolished. The other apse is not even mentioned, but it is quite reasonable to venture the opinion that the apsidal group showed originally all its unity, as is now the case of the «twin» church of St.Lawrence.

The tall nearby wall is what remains of St.Michael Fort, whose construction also affected the church itself. According to two agreeing documents by Antonio Campi (1523-1587) and Pellegrino Merula, usually well-informed chroniclers, Bernabò Visconti fortified and enlarged the Fort, enclosing the church in it, in 1369, the year of St.Gregory's foundation (as we see, this church's history is always intertwined with the parish church of St.Michael). As a result of the Fort's enlargement the parish priest was forced to live temporarily in the subsidiary church till at least 1401, as proved by a document. After the French destroyed the stronghold in 1521 it was rebuilt in 1553 by the Spanish who joined it to the sacred building demolishing the old St.Michael's gate, which was very close to the church, and opened a new one not far from there, which was called Roman Gate and would be demolished in 1910.

Walking close to the outer church side it is worth observing the narrow and elegant Romanesque one-light mullioned windows, unfortunately walled up during the second half of the 19th century in order to open graceless lancet windows. Perhaps during that same rash restoration attempt a small Oratory which had stood against the right side in alignment up with the façade since the 17th century, as is shown in an engraving of 1836, was destroyed.

Once we arrive in front of the façade, really a palimpsest after the several changes occurred through out the centuries, it is necessary to remember that, during the restoration begun in 1861 by the parish priest Carlo Tessaroli, the three-light mullioned window on the façade, opened during the 17th century, was suppressed and two two-light mullioned windows and two lateral rose-windows, previously replaced by rectangular windows, were opened. While we are talking about restoration, let us recall another unwise attempt carried out by the parish priest Angelo Bonati after the first one, initiated by Tessaroli, who spent the sum of 13,487 Lira received by the Austrians as compensation for the damages suffered in 1901 by the church and the priest's house because of a big fire which broke out in the sacristy and then into the choir and the presbitery, threatening to destroy the roof. After the fire, in fact, some traces of the original building had emerged, but unfortunately they were partly destroyed both along the walls and in the vaults of

St. Michael Vetere's: *interior.*

the lateral apses, while the ones in the central apse were left untouched. The parish priest Giovanni Varischi, succeeded to Bonati in 1911, initiated after a careful survey the restoration of the crypt that the Austrian troops had used as a cellar and store-room for munitions: Varischi had the walls scraped off, which brought to light the three windows of the central apse. Outside, the windows themselves, no longer visible because of an embankment hiding them, convinced restorers to carry out a radical digging up. Therefore, by lowering the road level, the only apse left was given a sense of slender verticality. Amid strong opposition among restorers themselves, works were also carried out in the church interior which was freed of the structures added from the 15th to the 17th centuries; moreover the old truss roof was replaced by vaults. It is therefore evident that it is impossible to reconstruct the original features of the old church on the basis of the Romanesque and Gothic fragments. In fact at the end of the 13th century the church was completely restructured, except for the apsidal area, and on that occasion the round Romanesque arches were turned into slender pointed arches in the Gothic style.

The façade is divided by four massive half-columns, as tall as the wall which stretches in its broadness arranged in harmonious surfaces. The central part is elegantly raised above by two half-columns grafted on the typical crown of cross-arches marking the slopes and the height of the aisles, and underlining horizontally, the coupled small open galleries above the prothyrum. The entrance door, with embrasures formed by a number of girders is framed by a prothyrum which seems more designed than real because of the slight projection of the pilaster-strips enclosing and strengthening vertically the proportioned width of the underlying portal. The brickwork structure, with the geometrical exactness of bricks arranged regularly on thin lime layers, seems more apt to enhance the pictorial effects of the warm colour of the stone than to underline the plastic movement of the mass.

The interior of the church of St.Michael, in spite of a diffused luminosity due to broad pointed windows opened during the last century, retains the graveness of a slow and solemn motion. The high aisles, resting upon slender marble columns ending in typical sculptured capitals, enhance the wide and rythmical movement of the pointed arches which gently draw our attention to the isolated presbitery over which the broad bowl-shaped vault hangs giving the whole structure a sense of mystical recollection. The vault is almost completely occupied by the majestic and terrifying representation of the **Judging Christ, with sword in hand**, and on his sides, shivering with fear, are **the small figures of the judged**, painted with a sharp narrative expressiveness, showing no stylistic or allegorical formalism but, on the contrary, frank motion and simple colouring. As this painting had to strike the imagination of the most

simple folks it was realized on purpose in a very clear and simple language, although the solemn figure of Christ still retains some of the typical Byzantine stylisms. Such a figurative tradition, although deriving from the early Romanesque art, lasted until the beginning of the 14th century, and it was in time influenced by different styles and local art schools.

Therefore scholars agree about the dating of this fresco, between the end of the 12th and the first decades of the 13th century.

As for the columns and the capitals of the church devoted to the warrior Archangel, it has been written, and it is still believed, that all this material could have come from previous build-

St. Michael Vetere's: *1. Apsidal bowl-shaped vault with Christ the Judge painted in fresco; 2. Triptych representing: the Nativity, in the middle; St. Leonard deacon, on the right; St. Theodora, on the left, by B. Campi; 3. Crucifixion with the Saints Catherine of Alessandria, John the Baptist and the client B. Persico.*

ings, perhaps from Roman ones. On the contrary, in the above mentioned study about the temple of St.Laurence, a welldocumented hypothesis suggests that «the morphology of the columns suggests classical proportions» and that the use of marble columns, frequent above all in Tuscany, replaced the round, massive brickwork pillars, typical of the early Lombard Romanesque art. The suggested dating for these elements does not go beyond the 12th century and we believe that it could be suitable for those in St.Michael as well. A rough execution and a taste for simplification in the Corinthian order make the capitals of St.Michael clear examples of that late Romanesque plasticity which, without even considering the classical rules of order, was pursuing a formal expressiveness equal to the wild vitality of the «Romance» languages.

The present arrangement of the lateral altars, inside deep arches opened during the 15th century, does not correspond any more to the original one as well as their denomination. On 17 September 1300, for example, Giovanni Panevino in his will established for his relatives to erect and decorate an altar, now destroyed, devoted to St.Niccolò in St.Michael Church. The first altars were followed by others until, at the end of the 15th century, the church underwent a restoration which gave the aisles an appearance more suitable to the taste of those days. In 1486, in fact, Pope Alexander VI granted indulgence to all those who gave alms for the restoration of the church. On the second altar, on the right-hand side when

2

3

entering, inside a very elegantly carved and gilded frame, perhaps by Paolo Sacca, is a triptych by Bernardino Campi (1522-1591), representing, in the middle **the Nativity**; on the right **St.Leonard deacon** and on the left **St.Theodora**, too often mistaken for St.Bernardino. Campi carried out this work in 1568 for the nobleman Gabriele Meli who was entitled to the right of patronage over the altar, then very close to the apsidiole of the left aisle: this is how Bishop Cesare Speciano, during his Pastoral Visit in 1599, and Antonio Maria Panni in 1762 remember it. Then comes the altar which, according to the report of Bishop Speciano, was devoted to St.John the Evangelist and showed then a splendid painting, different from the present one, representing **the Crucifixion with the Saints Catherine of Alexandria, John the Baptist and the client Brocardo Persico** who, in 1571, had commissioned the work to Giulio Campi (c.1505-1573). The painting remained in the chapel of St.Catherine in St.Dominic Church until 1869-70 when the chapel was demolished in order to make room for a worthless «pleasant corner of plants and flowers». Although the historical events concerning the chapel, erected for Michele Persico in 1478, have been reconstructed and a number of different names have been suggested for the authorship of the work, not all critics agree in attributing the painting to Giulio Campi, in the last days of his prolific activity. In fact the artist simply translated in this work, without much inspiration, formal solutions which had already been used.

At the first altar of the other aisle, to the right-hand side if we turn our back to the apse, at the sides of a conventional plaster simulacrum of the sacred Heart, are two valuable panels representing **St.Anthony of Padua** (on the right) and **St.Nicholas of Tolentino** (on the left). Bishop Cesare Speciano wrote in 1559 only that the altar was devoted to the above-mentioned Saints and that it was decorated with an «icona pulcra», i.e. a beautiful painting which probably corresponds to the two panels, now lying on both sides of a painting representing **Our Lady of Sorrows with the dead Christ on her knees**. Now, the central part of this triptych stands out on the following altar which shows seven small canvases representing **the Virgin's Seven sorrows**. In 1606 Andrea Mainardi, also called Chiaveghino (c.1550-1614), perhaps together with his nephew Marcantonio, painted these small works for the altar, which is devoted more precisely to the Blessed Virgin of Sorrows. When, in an undefined period, the dressed simulacrum of Our Lady of Sorrows was removed from the niche, which is now hidden by the panel of the Pietà, this painting was hanged there instead of the simulacrum. This fine work is still being attributed rather dubiously to differ-

ent artists and in the last few decades the names of several 15th century painters, also some from Cremona, have been suggested: from Antonio della Corna to Bernardino Ricca, from an unknown artist from Ferrara, to Pseudo-Bramantino and Alessandro Pampurino (c.1460-62-c.1522-23). Scholars do not agree on the dating of the three panels either; however all of them believe that the artist must have come from Ferrara and acknowledge the incisiveness of the design and the shaping of forms which give figures a deep dramatic sense and a vibrating expressiveness.

With the same uncertainties were attributed to the same author four tempera works representing the **Saints Anthony Abbot and Jerome**, over the left side door; on the opposite wall is the **Annunciation**. These tempera works were original-

St. Michael Vetere's: *1. Altar of Our Lady of Sorrows with the Virgin and the dead Christ on her knees, in the middle; 2. The Saints Anthony Abbot and Jerome, tempera paintings by A. Pampurino; 3. The crypt.*

3

ly the organ hinged panels of the suppressed church of St.Anthony Abbot and had been in St.Michael since 1762. The Ferrara resentful touch, particularly in the figures of the two saints, develops, in the scene of the Annunciation, into a pictorial lyricism of Venetian inspiration.

Going down one of the two lateral stairs we come into the *crypt*. The light piercing through the small apertures seems to shape the architectural structure, supported by two cumbersome pillars and by two rows of small columns, covered by small cross-vaults. Particularly interesting are the five Longobard capitals which, according to a recent study (1971), are to be dated back to the 7th century; the study attributes the capitals to a Celtic-inspired culture, by this time far from the voluted classical capitals and from the geometrical Byzantine pulvins. However, although they are not yet Romanesque capitals with evil-like foliage and monster-like figures, that small figure of a roughly stylized man reveals the traces of a not-yet-converted world which seemed to need more to be exorcized than baptized.

After several restoration works and the dedication of this holy place to the soldiers who died in the First World War no trace has remained of the three altars mentioned during the Pastoral Visit of Bishop Speciano in 1599. The right of patronage over the high altar devoted to St.Peter, in the middle of the central apse, belonged to the Priors of the Confraternity called «St.Michael's Charity» perhaps as a remembrance of the fact that on this very altar the head and the body of St.Gregory had once been laid. In 1148, in fact, as mentioned above, this Confraternity had donated the first reliquary for the Relics of the Martyr Saint still revered in the Oratory near the Cathedral. The Company of Our Lady of the Weeping, established in 1583 and joined to the homonymous Roman Confraternity in 1585, used to meet behind that very same altar. In the small apses are two simple altars, so humble that Mass was never celebrated there. The time had not yet come then when a massive wall supporting the bell-tower was to alter irremediably the quiet, harmonious architecture of this crypt.

St. Abbondio Church

A visitor coming into the rather deserted small square, named after the homonymous St.Abbondio Church, after going down via Amati or Lauretano lane will find in front of him the following buildings, arranged in a sort of a big right angle: the geometrical structure of the Loreto-Sanctuary (1625), the elegant and severe architecture of the church (16th century) close to the imposing, square outline of the Monastery of the Humiliati (1511). The harmonious and regular outlines of the two sacred buildings, although erected in different times, form a perspective of such unity that the contrast between them and the austere façade of the Cloister is underlined even more.

The original church devoted to St.Abbondio and the attached Monastery were allegedly assigned by Bishop Olderico to the Benedictines in the 10th century; the monks remained there till 1246, when the Humiliati took their place in the ancient group of buildings. In 1468 the old Romanesque church was rebuilt and enlarged; the same happened in 1511 for the Monastery and the Cloister. After the suppression of the Humiliati, a notarial document dated 12 March 1579 testifies of the presentation of the Papal encyclical in favour of the Regular Clergy of the Theatine Order. Bishop Niccolò Sfondrati trusted them with the care of the church and the cloister which were then restructured again, and it was not until 14

November 1591 that Bishop Cesare Speciano could consecrate the new place of worship.

Along the right side of the church, on the side looking away from the monastery, stood once a small cemetery enclosed by a wall and a portico with rusticated stone columns. Pilgrims used to sleep there, under the arcades. Today St.Joseph Chapel and the Loreto-Sanctuary — built for Count Giovanni Pietro Ala who, after obtaining permission from the General Town Council, wanted the building to be erected at his expense as a perfect imitation of the Holy House in Loreto — rise together along the right wall of St.Abbondio Church. The sacred image of the Black Madonna, still the object of worship, was solemnly transferred there from the nearby Cathedral on 1 May 1625 after the Loreto Virgin had been proclaimed patron saint of Cremona. Among the many precious gifts offered through out the centuries to the revered image is a golden medal donated by Philip IV as a sign of gratitude for the end of the 1630 plague, while only a memory has remained of a «beautiful cloth of gold brocade» for the altar, of a precious chalice and of many other gifts.

The cemetery and the arcades, dotted with a number of votive offerings, were demolished to

1. Lauretano Lane; 2. St. Abbondio Church; 3. Altar with St. Joseph's wooden statue, by the Cremonese sculptor G. Bertesi; 4. Madonna in Glory by Galeazzo Campi.

(c.1466-1525), also recalls both Perugino's models (a panel in St.Augustine Church) and the quiet visions typical of Vivarini and Bellini. The beautiful panel, recently restored, was donated to the church in 1805 by Marchese Antonio Lodi.

Through the chapel we come into the church which has a nave divided into four spans, with six open arches so that three altars could be placed on each side. In the barrel vault and in the lateral small vaulting cells above the round windows the painter Orazio Samacchini (1532-1577) from Bologna painted a Glorification of the Virgin full of elaborated themes, proportioning it to the existing architectonic structures; the work was therefore framed by geometrical squarings marked by cornices and made more precious by swags. In the first octagonal fresco, at the beginning of the nave, a **big Angel bears a scroll with the writing**: «Ecce Virginem super choros Angelorum exaltatam» (Here comes the Virgin, raised above the choir of the Angels).

This is followed by **the Crowning of the Virgin and the praise of her virtues** inside a square framework and translated into symbols partly derived from the Sacred Scriptures and the Loreto-

make room for St.Joseph chapel, and during the demolition works many of those votive panels were burned. All that started on 23 July 1674, when, according to a project by P.Giulio Cavalli, works began in the chapel which had once been fully frescoed for Count Giulio Schinchinelli by the painter Giuseppe Natali (1655-1720) from Casale Monferrato. In the niche of the recently built altar, is the beautiful wooden statue of *St.Joseph*, a work by the sculptor Giacomo Bertesi (1643-1710) from Cremona who finished it in 1693 for Marchese Cesare Vidoni. About ten years before the erection of St.Joseph chapel, namely on 18 September 1663, P.Giulio Cavalli himself finished the cupola of St.Asella chapel, in front of the Holy House of Loreto. The arrangement of the façade of the small Loreto Temple can be attributed to the same architect.

Inside the Sanctuary's entrance-hall, which corresponds to the above mentioned chapel, and over the altar frontal, as the altar itself has been removed to make room for the baptismal font, is a wooden group representing the **Holy Family** which had originally been placed on the sacristy's main pen. The work was carved towards the end of the 17th century by Giacomo Bertesi for Marchese Cesare Vidoni. On the right wall of the chapel devoted to St.Asella is hanged an altarpiece representing the **Virgin in her Glory**, a valuable work by the painter Galeazzo Campi (1477-1536) from Cremona. The artist, although showing influences by Boccaccio Boccaccino

4

litanies. In the last span Giovanni Battista Trotti, also called Malosso (1556-1619), completed the work interrupted by Samacchini by frescoing, perhaps helped by Ermenegildo Lodi (17th century) from Cremona, **the three Theological Virtues** and, on both sides of the central rose-window, the **Annunciation**, widely touched up and re-made in many parts by the painter Giovanni Battista Pagliari (1741-1816) between the end of the 18th century and the early 19th century. Malosso was instead confronted with a more difficult artistic task. Above the presbitery rises a cupola, not as high as usually these structures

St. Abbondio: *1. Church interior; 2.-3. Views of the cloister, in the style of Bramante; 4. Altar-piece: the Virgin holding the Child on her knees and the Saints Nazario and Celso at her side, by G. Campi.*

64

are, with a representation of **the Assumption of the Virgin**. This big fresco was the last work of the painter Giulio Campi (c.1505-1573) from Cremona, who however only carried out the sketch and perhaps only parts of it: in fact the Order of the Humiliati, who had commissioned the work was suppressed in 1571 and the painter himself died in 1573. Then it was up to Giovanni Battista Trotti to complete the grandiose work which was finished in 1594, three years after the consecration of the church.

In the pendentives of the cupola, with his unmistakable Mannerist style, Malosso realized the figures of **David, Solomon, Daniel and Job**.

The altar-piece is a valuable work by the painter Giulio Campi; it was painted in 1527 and is the first documented piece by this artist. **The Virgin with the Child on her lap, sitting on a high seat beside the Saints Nazario and Celso, while at the foot of the marble throne are some putti playing with the weapons of the two Martyr Saints**. The young author reveals in this painting all his inborn talent in organically mixing different cultural influences, from the archaizing ones of the Ferrara tradition to the Lombard features typical of Romanino and Moretto.

Through a side door of the church, on the left-hand side, we come into the *cloister*, traditionally considered «in the style of Bramante». It is undoubtedly one of the most beautiful monastic group of buildings still existing in the town, built in 1511 on commission for the Humiliati who, according to a plausible attribution, assigned the work to architect Bernardino De Lera from Cremona. The severity and moderation typical of the style of Bramante in this architectural masterpiece are undeniable: in it the use of brick-material allowed the shaping of elements to take place and which seem more sketched than sculptured. The architect chose also to avoid sharp projections as well as undefended juts, thus preferring a decoration based on colours on which the light plays a game of limpid and calm beauty.

Fodri Palace

The monumental façades of different palaces are lined up almost close to one another starting from Venice Gate and going down along Matteotti Avenue: Cavalcabò Palace, widely renovated towards the end of the 18th century; Pallavicino Palace, built in Neoclassic style by Luigi Voghera, probably according to a project by Faustino Rodi, and Fodri Palace which belonged once to the homonymous family. The Fodri family had in fact grown rich thanks to a flourishing trade during the last years of the rule of the Sforza family in Cremona. Therefore their palace stood for a time

1. Fodri Palace; 2. Arcade and façade giving onto the courtyard; 3. Terracotta decoration, details; 4.-5. Fodri Palace: Bianca Maria Visconti and Francesco Sforza: tablets and lacunar ceiling.

5

when they were better off and the Fodri symbols of the counter or the merchant company were replaced by coats of arms.

In 1488 Benedetto Fodri commissioned to the sculptor Giovanni Pietro from Rho the family armorial bearings and a series of eight well-carved columns for a new arrangement of the palace's elegant courtyard. Six more columns were soon commissioned to Niccolò from Porlezza but unfortunately they are now lost. During 1490 alone the enriched merchant drew up a contract with

architect Guglielmo De Lera from Cremona for a radical enlargement of the medieval buildings belonging to the Fodri family.

The changes carried out by De Lera are probably to be seen in the idealized pureness of the façade, a typical example of Lombard Renaissance style, and above all in the arrangement of the asymmetrical sides of the courtyard for which he developed an indefinite open gallery on two tiers and on which shadows were broken by light columns and by the brickwork decorations of the pilaster-strips, according to the local tradition. In spite of the professed nobility of forms, the use of brickwork *friezes*, by Raynaldo de Stavoli or de Stauli, the *busts* modelled by Agostino Fondulo for the façade, the graceful *entrance portal*, sculptured by Alberto Maffiolo from Carrara and the *frescoes* by Antonio del Corna in the lunettes and the vaulting cells of the vestibule, the Palace retains its nature of a farmhouse raised to nobility, with its storehouses, cellars and store-rooms according to the wishes of the noble client.

On 6 November 1577, as proved by a notarial document drawn up by Giacomo Vitali, the Benedictine nuns of St.Mary in Valverde bought the Palace and used it as their Convent until 1748. Two years later it became the seat of the Monte di Pietà (Pawnshop) which occupied it till 1930 when it was bought by the Cassa di Risparmio delle Province Lombarde (Savings bank of the Lombard provinces).

SECOND ROUTE

SS. Marcellinus and Peter Church

Within the regular layout of four roads (Felice Cavallotti, Amilcare Ponchielli, Attilio Boldori and Carlo Rigotti) stands a majestic quadrilateral which encloses SS. Marcellinus and Peter Church and the College of the Jesuits attached to it. The powerful left side of the church is in fact prolonged without interruption up to the façade of the College, the only surviving evidence of the educational activity of the Fathers of the Society of Jesus from 1600 to 1773. An interesting exchange of letters between the noble widow Margherita Torre Ferrera, Isabella Berinzaga, the spiritual daughter of the Provincial Father of the Company of Jesus, father Achille Gagliardi from Cremona, the Jesuits

Bartolomeo Cigola and Agostino Fagnano and Bishop Cesare Speciano reveals the historical reasons for the arrival in Cremona of the Jesuits. On 24 January 1593 the noblewoman Margherita, after entering the Monastery of St.Martha, donated to the Jesuits her own house, completely furnished, and 1050 imperial Lire which could be asked to Count Giovanni Pietro Ala on condition that the Jesuits build a College in town. Fathers Bartolomeo Cigola and Carlo Spinola, already in Cremona in 1596, settled once and for all in the town where they officiated at the small church «of the Crib». In 1600 abbot Niccolò Amidano renounced his post as rector of New St.Michael Church which was assigned the following year to the Jesuits by Bishop Speciano. The following year, on 19 September, Giovanni Battista Piovano, town crier of the Commune, made public the

news of the noble widow's donation and affixed in the Communal Palace a copy of the notarial deed. Before the works for the College were to start, Bishop Cesare Speciano laid the foundation stone of SS.Marcellinus and Peter Church and a group of houses, bought by the bishop, were demolished so that the church and the College could be erected as one building. It was then that New St.Michael Church and the Church of the Crib disappeared.

Although the holy place was finished by 1625, the imposing building site still remained operating for a long time, so that the Jesuits had to use the whole sums donated by the noblewoman — the testament was drawn up on 24 May 1610 —, by Bishop Speciano, who died in 1607, and by other noblemen from Cremona. The church, solemnly consecrated by Bishop Giovanni Battista Brivio in 1620, received as a donation, during that same year, a part of the relics of the saints after how it was named; in 1622 the first important celebration was held in the church for the canonization of St.Ignatius Loyola. Only a large fragment of the canvas painted by Carlo Natali (1586-1683) and almost forgotten behind the high altar is what remains of that magnificent array. On that occasion Natali also painted the picture for the altar devoted to St.Ignatius (2nd chapel to the left), later replaced by another painting on the same subject by Angelo Innocente Massarotti (1654-1723). The wide nave, consistent with the scheme of a «con-

gregational church» with four deep apertures at the sides, each one containing a chapel, has two big wooden «anconas» in the transept which, by dilating the space, represent a balancing element for the presbitery. The solemn atmosphere of the architectonic spaces of the temple is pervaded by a stylistic severity which does not yield to Baroque temptations but, on the contrary, fits perfectly in the austere spirituality of the Fellows of St.Ignatius. The only notes of frivolous elegance are the *stucco works* which, by starting from the capitals, wind up along the cornice for the whole perimeter of the nave thereby separating the unfinished barrel vault from the multicoloured decoration of the chapels. According to existing documents, Giovanni Battista Boffa (1601-1674), who along with Carlo Natali is also to be mentioned, is the author of this valuable decoration which, without contrasts, covers the architectonic structure of the church. In addition, from a note written by Giuseppe Bresciani, we get the exact dating of the work: «the stucco work decoration in the church of the Jesuit Fathers, from the four chapels onwards, was finished» on 30 August 1652.

This dating is consistent with the one marked on the two **episodes from the life of St.Ursula**, on both sides of the wooden statue representing Our Lady, and also with the suggested dating of the painting of **the Presentation of Mary to the temple**. These three works are by Luigi Miradori, also called Genovesino. The two valuable panels were originally arranged in a different way: in fact, under the primitive altar devoted to the Virgin were once several relics, among which «five heads and twenty-two bones of the Virgins of St.Ursu-

---

1. Piazza Cadorna; 2. St. Peter and Marcellinus Church; 3. Interior; 4. Altar-piece of Mary Immaculate, by G.B. Bertesi.

la». When the big wooden altar-piece was finished the Saint Relics were placed beside the niche of the Virgin and the precious panels by Genovesino were used as two doors for the niches. Given their unsuitable position it is no longer possible to appreciate the picaresque narrative style animating that intense line of gestures and flashes of light both in the single figures and in the agitated groups of people.

In front of the painting of the **Presentation to the temple** painted by Genovesino is a humble picture signed and dated by Pietro Martire Neri (1591-1661), representing **St.Luigi Gonzaga who, an Angel on his side, renounces his title of marques**. On the right side, towards the exit, is a chapel devoted to St.Ignatius. Another personality of average talent, Giovanni Battista Natali (1630-1700), the son of Carlo Natali, painted in this chapel, in 1669, two episodes from the life of the Jesuits' founder: **St.Ignatius writing the Spiritual Exercises, and St.Ignatius freeing two possessed women**. As already mentioned later on a painting by Angelo Innocente Massarotti, an exuberant and fertile artistic figure in the local Baroque style, replaced the altar-piece by Carlo Nata-

li. The altar-piece of the following chapel, once devoted to the Transfiguration of Christ,is by the same author. The two most significant works by Massarotti, however, are the big square panels beside the high altar representing **the SS. Marcellinus and Peter flying in aid to the Cremonese army during the battle against the Milanese and the transfer of the Relics of the two Saints from St.Thomas Church into the Cathedral**.

The beautiful carved frameworks are the elegant creations of Giacomo Bertesi (1643-1710), the author, among other things, of the very elaborate foliage interlacery which decorates in the middle the primitive altar-piece, according to a late-Mannerist taste.

If such a sober framing was suitable for the painting by Gervasio Gatti (1550-1630), dated around 1604, it was considered on the contrary too bare at the end of the 17th century when the interior of the church was taking on the typical sumptuous features of the Baroque style. Giacomo Bertesi reused the architectonic structure of the primitive altar-piece after changing the position of the lateral columns in such a way that the overlying volutes were turned outwards. So,

around the austere painting by Gatti he carved, showing much inventiveness, that luxurious gilded foliage which soon became the distinguishing feature of his style and of his busy workshop. Moreover, he completed the upper part of the ancona with winged caryatids ending with volutes so that they could be better connected to the slender curls turned outwards.

The tireless artist from Cremona also realized the *crowning of the two confessionals*, one of which is preserved in St.Augustine church, *the pulpit*, the *frontal of the altar of St.Ignatius* (2nd chapel to the left) and the *chancel*. These works show a rich and well proportioned carving, also soft in the putti's heads and foliage, on which light creates pictorial effects. Given the size of the present publication we cannot discuss thoroughly the educational activity carried out by the Jesuits in the attached College. The building, still the seat of schools and offices, has been so radically changed that any attempt to reconstruct the

original structure would prove vain. However, documents prove that architect Francesco Pescarolo (1609-1670) built some halls for the Congregation of Noblemen soon followed by the Congregation of Merchants.

After the suppression of the Jesuits (1773) the Conventual Friars officiated at the church till 1798, when the Barnabite Fathers succeeded them and held it until 1810. In 1811 Saints Marcellinus and Peter Church ran the risk of being transformed into a riding school.

St. Lucy Church

Going down via Gaetano Cesari while coming from the church of St.Peter on the Po, and entering via Ruggero Manna, we come in front of the small apse of St.Lucy Church, commanded over by the massive and short bell-tower on its left.

The area on which this small Romanesque church rose in the 12th century was near the Medieval walls and the Po Gate, the present Piazza della Libertà (Freedom Square). The alleged founding of the church by Queen Theodelinda in

---

St. Marcellinus: *1. The Saints Marcellinus and Peter lead the Cremonese army to victory, by Angelo Massarotti; 2.-3. The Saints Marcellinus and Peter's funerals, by A. Massarotti.*

621 seems a rather unreliable hypothesis, while it is more probable that the foundation date is around the 12th century. In fact, the architectonic structures of the apse and the bell-tower clearly recall the Romanesque time. As was the case for a number of sacred buildings in Cremona (St.Abbondio Church, St.Omobono Church and St.Vincent Church) St.Lucy Church was also widely renovated in the 16th century, namely after 1583:during that year the Fathers of Somasca, previously officiating at St.Geroldo's, settled in the church after the renouncement of Cristoforo Brumano who had in the meantime become a «penitentiary» in the Cathedral.

A Cloister attached to the church was also built; it was bought by Marchese Persichelli after 1798, when the Congregation of Somasca was suppressed. The historian Giuseppe Grasselli (1818) reports that the Cloister was finished in 1642 after a project by Giuseppe Dattaro (1540-1619) who allegedly also renovated the façade of the church. The construction works in the Cloister, begun in 1604, lasted a long time, as is proved by several agreements between the master builders Bartolomeo Rinaldi from Como (1611 and 1623), Recanati (1629), and Iacobino Bergone (1634 and 1637) and the Fathers of Somasca. In 1622, at the request of General Father De Domis, architect Francesco Bigallo, also called Fontanella, was asked to assess the fabric's expenses perhaps because of a quarrel between the Fathers and the architects. The name of Pizzafuoco, undoubtedly corresponding to Giuseppe Dattaro, is mentioned only once. In fact a quite recent hypothesis suggests that the façade is a work by Francesco Dattaro and not by Giuseppe Dattaro: Francesco,

however, was already dead in 1576, seven years before the succession of the Congregation of Somasca to Cristoforo Brumano in the pastoral care of the parish. Moreover, an interpretation of the formal elements constituing St.Lucy's façade leads us to confirm Giuseppe Dattaro as their author. In the lower area, slightly projecting pilaster-strips are to be found, running together and interrupted, at the first tier, by the marked projection of the cornice, surmounted in its turn by other couplings of pilaster-strips which enclose the big contour of the rose-window.

To the sober elegance of the façade corresponds, inside, an unpretentious simplicity which is made lively by some paintings of a certain value. Among them we would like to mention an altar-piece by the Milanese painter Giovanni Antonio Cucchi, whose price was 35 sequins and which was placed in the second chapel on the right in 1748 together with six more small paintings, now lost, which represented the **Life of St.Gerolamo Emiliani**. Another valuable work is the altar-piece for the high altar, by Angelo Innocente Massarotti (1654-1723), one of the most brilliant figures in the Baroque painting school of Cremona. Finally, in the apsidiole at the end of the small left aisle are interesting remains from 13th century frescoes and a **Crowning of the Virgin** to be dated back to the first half of the 15th century.

1. St. Lucy: presbytery and High Altar; 2. St. Lucy: frescoes from the 13th century; 3. Ponchielli Theatre.

The Ponchielli Theatre

After leaving St.Lucy's we turn down via Angelo Morsenti until we enter Victor Emmanuel avenue where the Neoclassical Theatre stands which is now dedicated to the composer Amilcare Ponchielli (1834-1886) from Cremona stands.

The first theatre in the town ever recorded dates back to 1670 and was built according to the wishes of Giulia Ariberti, the sister of Archbishop Giovanni Battista and the wife of Marchese Osimo Goldoni Vidoni. It was however a private theatre where only noble people were admitted by personal invitation of the Ariberti family. In 1714, after the acceptance of a high inheritance, the «Filo Drammatico» theatre (in Piazza Filodrammatici — Amateur actor Square — near the public gardens) was turned into a church assigned to the Priests of the Oratory Congregation, commonly known as Fathers of St.Philip.

So, in 1747, Marchese Giovanni Battista Nazzaro had another theatre built according to a project by the painter and scenographer Giovanni Battista Zaist (1700-1757), calling the new, wooden building *Teatro Concordia*. The theatre, one of the first public entertainment halls in Italy after the Fenice in Venice and the S.Carlo in Naples, was inaugurated in 1749 during carnival time. The property of the building was transferred towards the end of the 18th century to a company of Cremonese noblemen. During the night of 11 September 1806 it was destroyed by a ruinous fire and the reconstruction, which lasted only sixteen months, was assigned to the Milanese architect Luigi Canonica who had just recently finished the Teatro Carcano in Milan, and to the master builder Francesco Mina from Cremona.

Theatres represented then for the middle-class society which had arisen out of the Revolution,

models of the Greek temples, Luigi Canonica planned his theatre following the example of the Scala of Milan, even though with a more moderate classical style. The interior was soon changed: in 1811 the stage was rebuilt by Faustino Rodi; in 1824 Rodi himself and Luigi Voghera realized a new roof as the previous one had been destroyed by a fire, and the last radical restructuring was carried out in 1930. The curtain, representing **Music** in all the different forms taken throughout the centuries, was painted by the Cremonese Antonio Rizzi (1869-1940) thus replacing another one by Giovanni Bergamaschi (1828-1903). The spectacular work by Rizzi was inaugurated in 1892, when the works for the iron bridge on the Po river were finished.

a set meeting point where richly decorated officers, diplomats in braided uniforms or haughty imperial officials entertained elegantly dressed ladies. This is why the new Teatro Concordia took on the form of a hall with boxes, with a more sober decoration in which the gilding typical of the 18th century was sensibly less and the whiteness of the classical elements more used. Therefore, by drawing inspiration from the classical

1. Ponchielli Theatre: interior; 2. A. Ponchielli, a portrait by V. Bignami exhibited in the Municipal Museum; 3. Church of St. Peter on the Po.

74

Church of St. Peter on the Po

Via Gaetano Cesari runs along the right side of the Teatro Concordia, now dedicated to Amilcare Ponchielli (1834-1886). The road goes at first slightly uphill and then in an even course arrives to the parvis of the 16th century Church of St.Peter on the Po.

According to a well-known Cremonese legend, the town owes the foundation of its sacred buildings, or their rich furnishings, to the devout wishes of a rich married couple. Likewise, the Church of St.Peter on the Po originated allegedly in 1064 and it gradually represented a motive force for the reclamation of that low-laying area which was then frequently flooded by the Po river. The Benedictine Monks who came there in 1068 and were skilful in hydraulic techniques and farming, reclaimed the surrounding fields by turning them into arable land. After them came, in 1439, the Canons of St.Mary Fregionaia who, in the same year, received by Eugene IV the title of Congregation of the Lateran Saviour, so that they are now commonly known as Lateran Canons. The Benedictine Abbot Cristoforo de Rubeis, unable to restore church and cloister alone, ceded the parish churches of St.Peter and St.Salvatore to the Lateran Community, which was willing to take on itself the responsibility of restoring the buildings and paying for the abbey's debts; Abbot De Rubeis reserved the right to an annuity of 50 florins. The agreement was confirmed on 24 June 1439 by Pope Eugene IV.

The new religious Congregation was then charged with the cloister's rebuilding and the res-

tructuring of the original place of worship which, during the Gothic period, had already been renovated on many occasions as can be seen on one side of the cloister and in the lower part of the bell-tower. How the outside of the Church of St.Peter on the Po looked like towards the end of the 15th century, after an enlargement carried out according to a new plan, can be imagined by observing a tarsia carved by Platina between 1482 and 1490 for the Cathedral's choir.In it, the foreshortened façade openly reveals the large background surfaces marked by slightly projecting pilaster- strips, the two lateral round windows and the big central rose-windows, according to the typical architectonic solutions suggested in those days by the De Lera family. The interior, on the contrary, was formed, according to Bresciani, by only one nave and a series of communicating chapels instead of the today's aisles, as can still be seen in St.Sigismund Church.

Local historiographic sources agree almost unanimously on the fact that Colombino Ripari, Superior of the Lateran Community, initiated in the 16th century the difficult enterprise of the above-mentioned rebuilding works and commissioned to master builder Agostino da Covo from Mantua the realization of his own project. On 25 August 1563, two days after the agreement be-

tween Ripari and the master builder, excavations for the foundation began and the first stone was laid on the 31st of the same month. The beginning of works is actually to be dated back to about ten years earlier, when, on 6 September 1555, Colombino Ripari commissioned to Gaspare Cairano from Brescia fourteen pilasters with Corinthian capitals according to a drawing by Giuseppe Sacca, a Cremonese carver considered a «reasonable architect» by Antonio Campi (1523-1587). Gaspare Cairano was to finish the work the following year. Works were going on

St. Peter on the Po: *1. Interior; 2. Ancona of the High Altar with altar-piece by A. Campi representing the Virgin with Child and Saints (1575) and wooden choir by G. Sacca (1564); 3.-4. Frescoes of the left transept and of the vault, by A. Campi.*

2

3

4

very rapidly, so that in 1556 the noble Fodri family was assigned an almost finished chapel in St.Peter's. A second work, important for the decorative layout of the church, commissioned in 1568, was the frescoing of the whole vault, the counterfaçade and the choir's walls. The artists asked to carry out the decoration were Cristoforo Rosa and Lattanzio Gambara from Brescia (c.1530-1574) who, most probably, did not finish the work. Meanwhile Giuseppe Sacca had already completed the refinedly carved wooden *choir*.

That first renovated building, after a ruinous collapse occurred in January 1573, was radically changed by a second project demanded by the Lateran Canons and their Superior Eusebio who, on 7 May 1573, ordered master builders Antonio Torre, Nicola Noce and Francesco Capra, to demolish the whole façade, the walls and the vaults over the chapels, including the vaults of the choir and the sacristy. From then on St.Peter's was no longer to be changed: it was divided into a nave and two aisles, with a large transept supporting a high dome, and a narrow and long presbitery stretching into the semicircular apse.

The above mentioned contract of 1573, although very detailed about the works to be carried out by master builders, does not even mention the architect who was in charge of the works. Therefore the name of Francesco Dattaro, who died in 1576, is suggested on the basis of stylistic and formal comparisons with other works signed by him or considered as his, such as the façade

of St.Abbondio's, of the Affaitati Palace, SS.Margherita and Pelagia Church and the chapel of the Blessed Sacrament in the Cathedral. The extended luminosity of the façade, subdivided by the strong projection of the cornice, is a clear mark of the harmonious and balanced intellectualism typical of the Cremonese Mannerism. The lower part, marked by coupled pilaster-strips, repeats in the front — which is enlightened by a large window in the style of the architects Sangallo and Palladio — the coupling of the pilaster-strips rising from the high base, and shows an elegant portal as the only element in relief which corrugates the flat, plastered surface. The portal was built by the stone carver Sebastiano Nani (? -1587) to whom the façade marbles were also commissioned.

The interior, perhaps because of the attempt to preserve some elements of the first reconstruction project, looks too narrow if compared with the length and the height of the sacred building, and yet it rightly applies the measured simplicity envisaged by the Council of Trent and ordered by St.Carlo Borromeo in the Milanese Synods. As for the *ornament of white and gold stucco works*, it is worth mentioning the frequent collaboration between Francesco Dattaro and the stucco worker Giovanni Battista Cambi, the best known member of this very active and large family. A notarial document dated 23 February 1580, however, attributes the plastic decoration of the nave and aisles to Brunoro Cambi. The above mentioned date is perfectly consistent with the Latin inscription written on the vault of the north wing of the transept: «Antonio Campi, who was the first to ornate these two vaults began working in 1579». Therefore not only were stucco works conditioned by the architectonic structure, but also, and even more, by the pictorial decoration.

The two wings of the transept were frescoed by Antonio Campi (1523-1587) who represented there **some episodes from the life of St.Peter** all of them, except for one, from the Acts of the Apostles. In the north wing he represented: **St.Peter receiving the servants of Centurion Cornelius; St.Peter praying by Thabita's death bed and Centurion Cornelius being baptized**, and in the south wing: **St.Peter and Simon the Magitian: the healing of the crippled before the temple's door; St.Peter before the Sanhedrin; St.Peter's release from prison**. It is a beautiful decoration in which Campi developed a blonde luminosity

well mingled with the stucco work gildings thereby realizing a work of a splendid mannerism which is also warmer and freer, though respectful of the rules of the classical drawing.

Similarly, a beautifully rich painting, which at the same time shows a high degree of self-satisfaction, is displayed in the vault of the nave: for it the names of Giovanni Battista Trotti, also called Malosso (1556-1619) and of his most brilliant pupil, Ermenegildo Lodi, are suggested based on uncertain reference notes.

Starting from the transept, in the middle of the first span is **Charity towards God**; on the right, **St.Peter's vision in Joppe**; on the left, **St.Peter walking on the waters**. On the following one, in the middle, **Charity towards your neighbours**. In the middle of the third span: **Faith**; on the right, **Jesus speaking from Peter's boat**; on the left, **the healing of Peter's mother-in-law**. In the next one,

1.-2. *The Saints Peter and Paul's flagellation and the Decapitation of St. Paul (1607) by G. Lamberti; 3. Nativity by Bernardino Gatti; 4. Martyrdom of Pope Alexander with the Saints Evenzio and Teodulo, a detail of a canvas by Jacopo Ferrari (1658).*

in the middle: **Temperance**. Finally, in the middle of the fifth span: **Fortitude**; on the right, **Peter's testimony in Philip's Caesarea**; on the left, **Peter before Christ after the miracle of the fish catch**.

The careful decoration works lasted until about the early 17th century. An almost unknown painter, Giorgio Lamberti, marked his name and the date (1607) on the springer of the cupola while frescoing the animated scene of the **Last Judgement**: the date, however, is not consistent with two payments in favour of a certain Orazio Lamberti dated 1603. Leaving scholars and critics to discuss this dating problem, we are inclined to attribute to Giorgio Lamberti the frescoes of the vault of the presbitery and of the apse's bowl-shaped vault representing the other episodes from the life of St.Peter, i.e. not the ones reported in the Acts of the Apostles but those handed down by tradition. In the middle of the apse is a monumental altar-piece which, according to a very recent and reasonable hypothesis is attributable to Antonio Campi, the imaginative inventor of all the elaborate devices realized in the last decades of the 16th century to celebrate famous personalities who came in visit to town. The first altar-piece, by Boccaccio Boccaccino (c.1466-1525) was replaced in 1557 by the **Nativity**, painted by Bernardino Gatti, also called Soiaro (c.1495-1576). The reason for the replacement is to be found in the traditional Nativity scene itself:

4

3

in fact, among its characters, in the foreground beside the Apostle Peter, is Colombino Ripari, responsible for the first rebuilding of the church in the 16th century. The valuable work by Gatti, which is now on the second altar to the left, on entering the church, was stolen by the French in 1797 and remained in France until 1814, when it was given back. The present altar-piece, which was placed here around 1800, represents **St.Catherine's mystic marriage and the SS.Vittore, Cataldo, Giustina and John the Evangelist** and was painted by Antonio Campi in 1575 for the high altar of the suppressed church of St.Vittore. The painting shows very clearly the high level reached by the painter in re-elaborating the Mannerist models of his brother Giulio while transposing them with expressions nearer to the Lombard naturalism.

On both sides of the altar-piece are two big canvases: on the right, **Pope Urban I baptizing St.Valerian**; on the left, **St.Ambrose baptizing St.Augustine**. The former, signed and dated (1665) is by Giovanni Battista Natali (1630-1700) who in 1657 also painted the elaborate scene of the **martyrdom of St.Thomas of Canterbury**, placing it on the right wall of the transept. The two enormous canvases on the side walls of the presbitery are also worth mentioning: they were painted in 1657 and in 1658 by Giacomo Ferrari from Mantua and represent **the martyrdom of SS.Alexander II,**

cently restored (1980) fresco can be seen representing **Christ's Circumcision**, a significant work by Giulio Campi (c.1505-1573). On the last altar, near the entrance door, is a canvas by Giovanni Battista Trotti, also called Malosso, representing **the Virgin with Child and St.John the Baptist and the Apostle Paul**. Opposite, in the right aisle, is another painting by the same author dated 1583 and representing **the SS.Francis and Bonaventura in adoration of the God's name**. Malosso, with his easy but educated and refined eclecticism, was able to create in this work an atmosphere with cold toned, pearly hues, particularly in the «whispering» scene in the woods which stands in contrast with the red and golden tones of the celestial apparition. The two canvases come from the demolished church of St.Angel. Two more paintings bear the signature of this versatile and fertile representative of the Mannerism, the former being **the Nativity** (4th altar to the right) and the latter is to be found on the altar devoted to *St.Mary of the Egyptians*. A document of 1573 recalls that instead of today's right wing

Evenzio and Teodulo; and **St.Guerrino, a Lateran Canon, giving alms**. Some ideas inspired by the works of Genovesino, e.g. in the group of beggars waiting for the alms, do not succeed in eliminating the feeling of impending heaviness aroused by the background architecture. Unfortunately we cannot discuss further the number of decoration works carried out in the church until 1880, when Giovanni Bergamaschi (1828-1903) frescoed 28 medallions with **episodes from the life of the Saints** and 56 ovals with **the Pope's portraits** on the internal sides of the pilasters.

Of the ten paintings placed on the corresponding altars of the aisles — we begin our visit from the right hand side when turning our back to the apse — and framed by precious altar-pieces of gilded and painted wood, we mention here the panel (2nd altar) signed and dated in 1524 by Francesco Bembo, representing **the Virgin with Child and the SS.Cosma, Damiano, Gerolamo and an offerer**. The painting, from the church of St.Angel, now demolished, is a proof of the period of cultural revival which spread rapidly in Cremona during the first decade of the 16th century. On the following altar is a painting by Antonio Campi (1567) which remained until 1789 in the Church of SS.James and Vincent, governed by the Barnabites who took the picture with them when, after the suppression of the Black Carmelites, they were transferred to the Church of St.Peter on the Po. Above, inside the altar-piece crowning, a re-

of the transept there was a chapel devoted to St.Mary. That building, according to Merula, must have been a small church and it was demolished during the enlargement which followed the rebuilding by Colombino Ripari. This altar was then erected to the memory of the old sacred place and a daily mass for the Dead was celebrated on it according to the legacy wanted by the Lateran Canon Marco Gerolamo Vida, later Bishop of Alba. On the third altar of the right aisle is an interesting panel of **Christ's Deposition** painted in 1521 by Bernardino Ricca who, although inspired by archaic models typical of the area around Ferrara, developed an idea by Raphael which had been popularized by the engraver Marcantonio Raimondi.

The big *cloister*, one of the most remarkable architectonic group of buildings of the 16th century in Lombardy, was erected over different periods of time by Cristoforo Solari, also called il Gob-

bo (the Hunchback), beside that part of the building which is directly connected to the church. It was turned into military barracks at the beginning of the last century and it was later divided up into private houses. Master builder Matteo from Prato, who signed the contract with the Abbot of St.Peter's on 2 July 1505, had to keep to a wooden model realized in Milan, provided that the client did not ask the original plan to be changed. Three years later, in 1508, Lorenzo de Trotti was asked to sculpture twenty marble columns, bases and capitals in order to finish the side of the cloister which looking towards the town walls. A third document dated 1522 mentioned an agreement between Abbot Ripari and the master builders Aaron de Finis and Giovanni Antonio de Fostinellis, in which it is stipulated that the fourth side of the monastery had to be finished by the following year. The result was a severe and moderate architecture in accordance with the austere character of the new Congregation of the Lateran Canons.

In the internal courtyard of the building, beside the church, the old refectory of the monks is still preserved, and there Bernardino Gatti, also called Soiaro, frescoed a **very crowded Miracle of the loaves**, thereby painting, with a marked taste for portraiture, a heterogeneous survey of men and women caught in the satisfactory gesture of eating that miraculously multiplied bread.

St. Peter on the Po: *1. Altar-piece by G. Bembo; 2. St. Mary of Egypt, a work by G.B. Trotti, also called Malosso; 3. Refectory wall: the Miracle of the Loaves, a fresco by Bernardino Gatti, also called Soiaro (1552).*

SS. Aegidius and Omobono Church

Along the present via Leonida Bissolati we turn down via Ruggero Manna at the cross-roads with St.Omobono lane, until we reach the isolated small square where St.Omobono Church stands: the sacred place was once devoted to St.Aegidius, so that old documents still report the denomination of: Parish Church — later Collegiate church, — of the SS.Aegidius and Omobono.

No trace has remained of the Medieval district, nor of Omobono's house itself which was transformed in 1605 into an Oratory in which a Confraternity having Omobono as its patron saint lived. The only memory left of that period is a memorial stone dating back to the 18th century now enclosed in an elegant marble portal decorating the façade of a modern palace. In front of the beautiful «proto-Baroque façade» of the church (1602), is a small square whose irregular cobbled paving covers a cemetery, mentioned by the Pastoral Visit reports, which was used as a pauper's communal grave during the 1630 plague when the town's population was reduced by a half. After going up via Ruggero Manna we turn left into via Colletta and, before reaching St.Augustine Square, we notice a recently built palace which has wiped out the last traces of the place where the Company of St.Omobono, an istitution which passed through the same events as those which affected the church, was once housed.

It is impossible for us to imagine how St.Aegidius Church must have looked in the days of the merchant Omobono Tucenghi, later patron saint of the town (1356), and it is also difficult to suggest hypotheses about the temple's planimetry. The only certain thing we know is that where the present St.Omobono Church stands there were previously two churches: the one devoted to St.Aegidius Abbot which Bresciani's and Balladori's memoirs date back to the days of Berengarius II King of Italy, namely to 7 May 949 when Diamberto Germano was Bishop of Cremona; and the other devoted to St.Omobono. The date of 949 for the original St.Aegidius's seems to be the oldest and the most reliable one if one thinks that under Olderico's episcopate, in 986, two churches, the former devoted to St.Laurence and the latter to St.Mary and the Apostles Philip and James, were rebuilt at the opposite end of the town outside the walls. The Lancetti manuscript, on the contrary, by giving a piece of information which is even less documented than the previous one, goes back to the year 513, when Bishop Grisogono Sardo divided the town into parishes and included St.Aegidius's among the parish churches.

Moreover it is also impossible to confirm the reliability of another document by Bresciani in which it is stated that Egidio Guiscardo, Bishop of Cremona, «commissioned the building of a Chapel for his own devotion, which he dedicated to the Holy Mother of God» in 958. Therefore, the testimony of a notarial act by Amilcare Tensino dated 1047 which attested that Ardengherio and Attilia Isolani, a married couple, furnished the parish benefice of St.Aegidius, although no trace has remained of it, is so far the most plausible one. The origin of the title of «Collegiate» given to the church for the first time in 1049 is lost in legend. A decisive date for the building activities of St.Aegidius's was 13 November 1197, when Omobono Tucenghi died during the celebration of a Mass. Two years later that «good man» (his very name, Omobono, means «good man») was canonized and that was only the official confirmation of a cult which would cause, from then on, all the renovations and the decorations of the temple until about 1805, when the small parish was joined to the nearby St.Augustine Church.

Among the events which followed the merchant Saint's death a date mentioned by Bresciani, 1202, is of particular interest: it was then that, as a result of the growing devotion for the saint, the body of St.Omobono was placed into a mar-

1. *Saints Aegidius and Omobono's Church; 2. Bishop Sicardo's statue; 3. St. Omobono's statue; 4. Interior.*

3

draw the readers' attention to the beautiful façade, a work dated 1602 by Giuseppe Dattaro (1540-1619), to the reconstruction of the lantern (1607-1618) and to a new altar devoted to St.Omobono (1616-1617). A marble altar-piece by the masters Bernardo Pozzi, Silvestro Gino and Giorgio Giorgioli from Merede (Lugano) was added to the altar «mensa» finished in 1615 by Matteo Galetto. As for the façade — divided in its lower part by coupled pilaster-strips interrupted, at the first tier, by the marked projection of the cornice which is surmounted in its turn by pilaster-strips marking the window in the style of Sangallo and Palladio — the touch of Giuseppe Dattaro, in his full maturity and already showing signs of a Baroque sensibility, is easily recognizable.In the niches beside the portal are two statues which (since 1647), had been thought to represent the *SS.Aegidius and Omobono*, year of the Pastoral Visitation of Bishop Francesco Visconti. A new hypothesis put forward in 1971 suggests that the statue in St.Aegidius's may represent Bishop Sicardo who died almost twenty years after St.Omobono (1215). The two sculptures, attributed to an «imitator of Antelami», reveal the influence of the «Master of the Prophets», the author of the works on the Cathedral's main portal, and of the anonymous «sculptor of the Months», which are lined up on the front of the Cathedral's prothyrum. The revered images of Omobono and Sicardo stand in between these two somewhat opposite figurative exemples and, although they

ble tomb. Moreover, on the left side of the present church an old, precious testimony can still be seen: an apsidiole which survived all restorations. Inside the temple a narrow and steep small marble stair corresponds to the apse: it was commissioned in 1601 by parish priest Biagio Rossi to leed down to the burial place of St.Omobono. The strong will to preserve the small apse and the nearby remains of a Late-gothic wall is explained by the fact that what survived of the joining of the old St.Aegidius and of St.Omobono Churches belonged most probably to the original building devoted to the merchant Saint. The Lancetti manuscript of the 18th century reports that the two churches «were razed to the ground» in 1363 in order to build a new one. However, although the thin thread of history still hides a number of events, the Cremonese historian is belied by the report of the Pastoral Visit of Stefano Bottigella in 1470 who visited first St.Omobono's and then St.Aegidius's. Moreover, Father Omobono de Bellintendi is mentioned on the report as the priest of the two sacred buildings. The same testimony, even if much later, was given in 1600 by Bishop Cesare Speciano during his visit to a church which was then already called SS.Aegidius and Omobono Church.

Given the size of the present guide-book we cannot examine all the restoration works carried out in the church by the Company of St.Omobono, founded in 1357, nor can we discuss the renovations which Bertolino Ongaroni, Bartolomeo and Giacomo De Lera carried out in the 15th century in the two churches; yet we would like to

4

have been worn out and made dull by time, which has gradually caused the colour of the red marble of Verona to fade away, they stand as severe witnesses of the Lombard-Emilian culture in the early 13th century.

Since its foundation in 1357 the Company of St.Omobono had always performed a kind of «patronage» function over the church but, in the early 18th century, it was forced to share it with the Counts of Marcignago of the noble Visconti family who did not miss any opportunity to munificently commission for it many works of arts. Count Antonio Visconti obtained in 1730 for his son Carlo, parish priest in St.Omobono's, the privilege of the mitre and the pastoral staff; in 1734 he commissioned to the goldsmith Pier Francesco Zucchi a new silver reliquary and had the whole church frescoed. The pomp of the great decoration which covered the whole interior of the church without leaving a single blank space turned out to be a very remarkable work also because it largely influenced the whole Cremonese artistic world. Figurative frescoes were commissioned to Giovanni Angelo Borroni (1684-1772), who probably collaborated with his son Vincenzo, while the spectacular quadraturas were painted by Giovanni Battista Zaist (1700-1757). As regards the dating of these frescoes, local historians have written since the 18th century that the lantern was frescoed in 1744 and the vault and the nave in 1753. A new document reports on the contrary that the Company of St.Omobono was asked on 17 June 1753 by the old Count Antonio Visconti to lend him «the tapestry to cover the boards which close the octagon» (the cupola) in order «to have it restored and painted». This testimony and the date are proved by the memoirs of the parrochial vicar, father Carlo Antonio Stefanoni. Finally, a memorial stone over the entrance door and a notarial act make it possible to state that the frescoes of the nave were finished

in 1754 and that the decoration in the aisles was also practically completed in 1755. Borroni's painting, although dealing with sacred themes, is more similar to scenes of profane allegory and to the elegance of a prince's palace, even if this particular effect is rather to be ascribed to Zaist's quadraturas.

On 27 August 1779, after Giuseppe Antonio Bottazzi, procurator of the Company of Blessed Sacrament in St.Omobono, had asked the Cathedral's Fabric to provide all the material necessary to the clean Borroni's paintings, the member of the Fabric Board replied that «the Orders of this eminent Fabric are against the cleaning». So, the great decoration by Borroni and Zaist has never been cleaned since it was first painted.

4

St. Augustine Church

On the area where the imposing group of buildings of St.Augustine's now rises, stood once the small churches of St.Thomas and St.James, the latter called «in Braida», being this the name given to the cultivated fields outside the town walls. A map of the town designed by Antonio Campi (1583) shows that the «old course of the Po river», which lapped Cremona then stretching almost to St.Peter's, ran in fact near St.Augustine Square, in the same district where SS.Aegidius and Omobono Church was built. Similarly, the nearby group of buildings of St.Benedict was also built «in Braida».

According to Merula's reports and to a testament in favour of the Augustinian community, the hermits of St.Augustine's, commonly called Au-

gustinians, had been living outside the town since 1254, at the parish of St.Fabian in a small village called «S.Maria del Riposo», before moving to this district. Some years later, in 1260, the monastery and St.Thomas Church were assigned to them together with some houses. The small church soon proved inadequate for them so that the Augustinians were allowed by Bishop Cacciaconte Sommi to build a new and a larger one. Before one century had elapsed, the monks asked Bishop Ugolino to be assigned the temple of St.James in Braida in order to demolish it on the ground that the construction prevented a further enlargement of their big architectonic group of buildings. This request is recorded by a notarial act registered on 27 January 1336.

Between 1339 and 1345 architect Teodosio Guarneri erected St.Augustine Church in Lombard-gothic style, with one nave and two aisles, without transept, with polygonal pilasters of brickwork and a rectangular apse. The typical features of the Gothic style are recognizable in the austere saddle façade, divided into three parts by thin half-column buttresses and lightened by the slender, pointed small arches of the gallery and in the marked verticalism of the cusp, more than in the interior which was radically changed in the 16th century. Moreover, it is to be noted that on the façade, consecrated on 7 March 1478, the signs of the restructuring carried out in the interior between 1553 and 1568 are clearly visible. As the roof was lowered in order to build a new barrel vault, the previous pilasters of brickwork were so

---

1. Adoration of the Magi, by G. Campi; 2. Dome with frescoes by Angelo Borroni; 3. General view with St. Augustine Church; 4. St. Augustine Church.

enlarged that they took on the form of a cross, obtained by adding four stout pilaster-strips; the Gothic central rose-window was also lowered while the two lateral ones, now closed by boards, were opened in a lower position; finally, the apse, after losing its original rectangular form, became semicircular. Shortly after the completion of works two wide chapels were opened beside the right aisle: the former, devoted to the SS.Relics, lies near the façade and the latter (in the row of chapels it is actually the third one), built according to the will of Ugolino Cavalcabò, Seignior of Cremona, was devoted to the Virgin. The marked and regular appearance of the quadrangular pilasters and the splayed and well outlined windows, which are elements shared by both buildings, suggest that the chapels may be dated back to a time between the end of the 14th and the first decades of the 15th century, when several families of architects and engineers, such as the Oldoini, the Ongaroni and the De Lera families lived and were active in Cremona. According to a fairly recent hypothesis the chapels of the SS.Relics and of the Blessed Virgin should be ascribed to an architect from Cremona named Montesono, who was also active in Brescia in the church of S.Maria del Carmine. Two more smaller chapels were built approximately in the same period beside the previous ones. A pointed window is to be seen walled up in the outside wall of the second chapel, called Passion chapel, in which the stucco worker Giovanni Battista Barberini, from the Intelvi Valley, represented in 1666 with plaster and stucco some scenes from the **Sorrowful Mysteries**. The window, the only surviving element after radical changes, fits in with the features of the above mentioned chapels. In the fourth chapel, which had been allegedly devoted to St.Ann since 1422 and is now devoted to St.Nic-

colò of Tolentino, it is almost impossible to recognize even the slightest trace of the old building. Therefore it is to be assumed that the chapel may have been completely reconstructed when, in the second half of the 16th century, every Gothic element in the interior was removed.

Vegetable gardens stretch now against the left side of St.Augustine Church, while the same space was once occupied by the *monastery with two cloisters* and an extremely rich *library* which was completely frescoed, at the end of the 16th century, by Giovanni Paolo Cavagna (1556-1627), Fra' Solecito of Lodi and Orazio Lamberti. Of the group of buildings only the majestic, quadrangular bell-tower, raised in 1461, still stands.

The interior of the sacred building although retaining solemn proportions does not possess any longer the slender Gothic verticality which would have made it to appear even more dilated, but shows on the contrary an altered ratio between nave and aisles and between the church's height and length. Moreover, the **twenty-four statues of Figures from the Old Testament and the Augustinian Saints**, modelled in stucco by the skilful, although not brilliant sculptor Giovanni Battista Barberini, which are supported by pilasters in the nave and in the aisles, have contributed to enhance that sense of oppressive heaviness already created by the 16th century structures. St.Augustine's also contains one of the best plastic works by Barberini, **the Mysteries of Christ's Passion** (2nd chapel on the right) which represents the same figures and stories found in the Pre-

1

Alpine Sacred Mountains. The sacred image, which wants to touch the visitor's soul, gives an over-emphatic representation of the character's psychology and choses an expressiveness which encompasses even the chapel's architectonic space.

Although it was severely damaged between 1736 and 1737 — when the vault was lowered, a new supporting brickwork was built against the lateral walls and an imposing marble altar-piece was placed close to the background wall — the decoration of the *Cavalcabò Chapel* (3rd chapel on the right) represents one of the most significant cycles in the Late-gothic painting of north-

ern Italy. The frescoes by Bonifacio Bembo, discovered in 1950, were given back only in 1963, after long and patient restorations, their delicate lyricism and precious colouring. In the apse's bays is a much damaged **Crowning of Mary**, enlivened by a pure hue which flows like a song inside the gracefully designed outline, marked by flowing lines. Along the underside of the arch dividing the apse's vault the **Virgin's Forefathers** are frescoed on a preciously arabesque background. In the vaulting cells **the evangelist St.Matthew** is represented together with **St.Jerome**; **St.Mark** with **St.Gregory Magnus**; **St.Luke** with **St.Ambrose** and **St.John** with **St.Augustine**. The Evangelists, sitting on sculptured thrones which look like miniature cathedrals, and the Doctors of the Latin Church were arranged by Bonifacio Bembo in a flow of a continuous figurative narration, only partly limited by the precious decoration themes which follow the silent flowing of forms. In the corner of the vaulting cells themselves are **Adam and Eve** innocent in their nakedness beside the **symbols of Earth and Fire**. This decoration, almost shadowless, in a warm throbbing of elegant lines and enamelled colours, was the extreme, bright expression of a courtly society which loved flowered ornaments and preciously decorated, fairy-like narrations. Finally, on the right wall, instead

1. Side of St. Augustine Church; 2. View of the nave; 3 Vault of Cavalcabò Chapel, painted in fresco by Bembo.

side of the altar. On 27 June 1740, at the age of 81 — the exact figure is important in the settling of a chronology dispute — the painter Sigismondo Francesco Boccaccino was buried here.

The *tomb of the astronomer*, mathematician and philosopher *Giovanni Battista Plasio*, who died around the age of ninety in 1497, is preserved in the chapel devoted to S.Niccolò of Tolentino. The valuable work is still being discussed by critics and it is ascribed to Giovanni Pietro of Rho by some and to Lorenzo de Trotti by others. Beyond this chapel, a panel bearing a *bas-relief* sculptured in 1357 by Bonino of Campione can be seen on the fourth pillar of the right aisle. The panel, coupled with another one, also

of the pictorial decoration which on overlapping tiers would have completely covered the chapel's surface, are **the portraits of Duke Francesco Sforza and Duchess Bianca Maria Visconti**, frescoed by Bembo on both sides of the altar devoted to the SS.Crisante and Daria.

It is worth mentioning here as a historical curiosity, that the heavy 18th century structures mentioned above were built according to the will of the Company of the Cinturati («belt-wearers») which had their tombs in this chapel, on the left

St. Augustine's: *1. St. John and St. Augustine, a detail of Cavalcabò Chapel; 2. Madonna with Child and pious Saints, bas-relief sculptured by B. da Campione (1357); 3. The Virgin with Child and the Saints Jacob and Augustine, by P. Vannucci, also called Perugino; 4. Dome of the Holy Sacrament Chapel with the Doctors of the Church.*

fixed on the last pilaster of the left aisle, belonged to a dismembered tomb which is now recognized by some scholars as St.Omobono burial place, even if this is not proved by any documents.

The three altars, after the said chapels, were decorated in 1663-1664 with Baroque altar-pieces by Giovanni Battista Natali (1630-1700) who would change the altars in the Cathedral some years later.

On the fifth altar is a panel by Pietro Vannucci, also called Perugino (1448-1523), commissioned by the noble Roncadelli family in 1494 and later ceded to the church as a perpetual deposit. The painting, stolen by the French in 1796, remained in France until 1818, when it was given back. It is undoubtedly one of the most interesting works in St.Augustine Church, both from an artistic and from a cultural point of view, and also as far as the development of the 16th century painting in Cremona is concerned. **The Virgin is sitting on a high throne with the Child in her arms beside the SS.James and Augustine.** The blurred luminosity of the background corresponds to a feeling of sincere poetry in which the figures of the Virgin, serenely sad, and of the Saints, in calm attitudes, are immersed.

At the bottom of the right aisle is the chapel of the *Blessed Sacrament*, once completely frescoed by Giovanni Pietro of Cemmo with **episodes from the life of St.Augustine.** The restructuring works carried out in the 16th century hid this significant pictorial cycle, found in 1820 and restored only in 1912. On the vault, the best preserved element of the whole group, are **four «oculi» in perspective from which the Doctors of the Latin Church,**

beside the symbol of the four Evangelists and the primordial elements: **Fire, Earth, Air and Water** stand out. On the underside of the arch are **the four Sybils.** Because of the late artistic flourishing in Cremona during the period of the Sforza family, in which the archaizing taste of courtly painting is mingled with the new language by Foppa and Amadeo, this work is thought to date back to the last decade of the 15th century.

Through a small, lateral door we come into the choir, overlooked by a monumental, carved and gilded altar-piece which encloses a picture of peculiar subject: **Christ under the press,** a work signed and dated in 1594 by Andrea Mainardi, also called Chiaveghino (c.1550-c.1614). A recent restoration, carried out in 1971, has allowed us to better understand some details of the painting: the press is the cross itself; a figure from the crowd is drinking from the chalices filled with the Divine blood and St.Gregory Magnus, among the Doctors of the Latin Church, is devoutly collecting the precious Blood flowing from a tap. Moreover, a wide fresco fragment, discovered behind the canvas, has been peeled off and is now preserved in the chapel of the Blessed Sacrament: the restoration has made possible to attribute the work to Chiaveghino and to date it back to 1577. It is the first documented work by a modest painter who, however, thanks to a tireless activity, was included among the group of good followers of Campi's style in the last decades of the 16th century. Perhaps because of a pathetic and sugary religious feeling the Augustinians commissioned to Mainardi four more paintings for their church, which were placed in the left aisle: **Jesus's Baptism (1593)** at the first altar; **the Virgin with Child and the SS.Catherine of Alexandria, Dominic, Augustine and Leonard (1585)** at the second; **the**

4

meeting of Joachim and Ann (1590) at the third and the Eternal adored by five Saint Women, at the last altar of this aisle.

On both sides of the presbitery and on the counterfaçade wall are three huge canvases by the Cremonese painter Angelo Innocente Massarotti (1654-1723), the most remarkable representative of the local Baroque taste. In this work, representing St. Thomas of Villanova building churches and giving alms (1689), at the right of the altar, although inspired by the gloomily shadowed figures by Genovesino, Massarotti soon modified his style, thanks to his brilliantly descriptive attitude, by shifting towards the dignified classicism of Rome and Bologna which turned the dark hues of the background into changing Baroque colours. In front of this painting, at the left of the altar, is another one narrating St. Augustine's conversion and showing an educated, academic classicism, more and more rarefied in the arrangement of its scenes and marked by bright colours which are made lighter and lighter. Finally, the large canvas over the entrance door does not represent St. Augustine telling the rule, as local historiographers have believed since the 18th century, but, according to a recent and reliable hypothesis, the Blessed Giorgio Laccioli from Cremona, founder of the Augustinian Congregation in Lombardy. It is therefore not an exaggeration, in our opinion, to consider this painting as Massarotti's masterpiece: in it he was able, unlike in his other works, to set a spectacularly theatrical scene, by animating it with a grandiloquent parade of noblemen and religious figures, portrayed by means of a refined painting technique which is almost a mixture of the realistic portraits by Genovesino, free from prejudices, and of the idealized portraits which, although keeping to naturalism, tried to show a celebrating emphasis.

SS. Margherita and Pelagia Church

If we turn right into via Guido Grandi after leaving St.Augustine Church and going down the narrow via Breda, we reach the most typical monument of the 16th century art in Cremona: SS.Margherita and Pelagia Church, commonly known as St.Rita.

The sacred building, surrounded on all sides by blocks of houses looking onto narrow streets, is to be observed from the corner of via dei Rustici in order to have a simultaneous vision of the façade, of the right side and of the bell-tower.

The historian Pellegrino Merula when writing about St.Margherita Church, mentions two important suburban monasteries: the former which belonged to the Lateran Canons and the latter, belonging to the Augustinian Canonesses, was devoted to St.Pelagia; Merula also tells us how the buildings were destroyed during wars. Therefore the rich rent coming from the two monasteries was assigned to St.Margherita Church which also took on the denomination of the martyr Pelagia of Antioch. The small church, perhaps because of such a rich income, became a Priory and when, in 1519, the famous humanist Marco Gerolamo Vida from Cremona (1470-1566), later Bishop of Alba, became Prior in SS.Margherita and Pelagia Church, the building was for the first time renovated in Renaissance style by Giulio Campi (c.1505-1573), perhaps helped by his brother Antonio (1523-1587).

On a high base are four pilaster-strips of brickwork framing the smooth surfaces of white stone of the façade and supporting a small architrave with a dedicatory inscription and a date: 1547. A projecting pediment, in the middle of which is the emblem of the Vida family, crowns a classical front which is balanced like a Greek temple. As no notarial documents about the construction of the temple are available, we cannot but rely on popular tradition according to which Giulio Campi was both the architect and the painter of frescoes in the church, even though the names of architect Francesco Dattaro (? -1576) and of Marco Gerolamo Vida himself, as the ones who inspired the overall architecture of the building and who chose the themes for the frescoes, have been recently suggested.

It is now worth mentioning that in 1535 the learned humanist Marco Gerolamo Vida published a Latin poem called «Cristiados» — a poetic narration of the life of Jesus — using the language in a very refined way, so that he was later called the Christian Vergil. Moreover, although he had been the Bishop of Alba since 1532, he returned to Cremona when the Monferrato war broke out and remained there for about a decade, from 1542 to 1552. The building of the church, and above all the whole internal decoration of SS.Margherita and Pelagia Church is therefore to be dated between 1535 and 1552. So, the artist Giulio Campi adapted and modified his inspiration and style following the perfect hexameters by Vida who, perhaps, suggested to the painter the episodes from the Bible as well as the evangelical scenes to be frescoed.

The scenes painted on the vault are in fact related to one another by a herudite iconography. In the big lunette, under the vault's intrados, is a **Crucifixion** to which, in the lunette over the entrance door, corresponds a **Resurrection** beside which are the **figures of Moses and David**, as the symbols of the Law and the Prophets, often quoted by Christ as a testimony for himself and his preaching. Two stories are frescoed on the first span of the vault, towards the counterfaçade: **David killing Goliath** and **Jonah expelled by the whale after three days**. Here the relation to Christ resurrected is clear: Jonah recalls to the evangelical prefiguration of the Resurrection and at the same time, David, by killing Goliath, symbolizes Christ winning over death. On the third span,

91

3

towards the presbitery, two more stories are frescoed: **Moses raises the bronze snake in the desert** and **the temptation of Joseph the Hebrew**. Here again the reference is to the Golgotha episode: the bronze snake prefigures the Crucifix raised on the mount. Similarly, Joseph who escapes temptations renouncing his mantle is the symbol of Christ on the cross who leaves only his body temporarily in the hands of death. Finally, in the central span, two episodes from the Book of Exodus are represented: **the fall of the manna** and **water flowing out of the rock**. The former refers to Eucharistic bread, and the latter, according to St.Paul's interpretation, to Christ identified in the desert rock from which water gushes out. So, here is the concept of the Eucharist as the representation of the Easter mistery and, perhaps, of Baptism which transforms people into Christians as the Christ himself by linking them to his death and resurrection.

The life of Jesus continues on the six, big lateral frescoes painted in the false arches on the walls, but it is logically completed with the episodes starting from the **Eternal in His glory surrounded by Angels**, represented on the small cupola over the high altar. God's plan to salvation is related to the **Annunciation**, painted on the counter-façade at both sides of the big rose-window, and enforced in the *Nativity* with the episodes of the

SS. Margherita and Pelagia Church: *1. Interior; 2. Triumphal altar-piece in the nave: Crucifixion, by G. Campi; 3. The falling of manna; 4. First span of the nave: David killing Goliath and Jonah being thrown back ashore by the whale.*

4

Adoration of the shepherds and of the Magi. These three different moments of the same narration are represented on the lower part of the apse. Then, starting from the presbitery, at the first lateral altar on the left is the **Presentation to the temple**, then **Jesus among the doctors** and **the preaching of Jesus**.

On the opposite side, near the entrance door, the evangelical narration goes on with **the Transfiguration, the Resurrection of Lazarus** and **the entrance of Jesus to Jerusalem**.

All these frescoes have been unfortunately badly damaged by dampness so that in 1920, on the initiative of the painter priest Illemo Camelli they were peeled off and reattached on canvas. The restoration was carefully completed in 1959. This was not really the first restoration attempt for Giulio Campi's paintings: in 1733, the painter Giovanni Angelo Borroni (1684-1772) and the quadraturista painter Giovanni Battista Zaist (1700-1757), ignoring the warning written at the request of Bishop Marco Gerolamo Vida on two panels at the entrance of the presbiterial arch — in which the «hatred and the revenge of the whole town» was called upon anyone who would dare to alter the balanced unity of the work — repainted the ornaments and even added new embellishments, made even more coquettish by multi-coloured garlands of flowers.

In spite of such a deplorable episode the shining decoration by Campi bursts out within the harmonious architectonic rhythm thereby revealing his different sources of inspiration: Pordenone, Giulio Romano, Correggio and Raphael. However, the overall style of the work is typical of Giulio Campi, who was able to merge different impressions into his personal taste and to create a noble and aristocratic language, full of learned quota-

tions and sometimes bordering on preciosity. His formal elegance and the high quality of his colouring place Giulio Campi among the most refined artists in the local Mannerism of the 16th century.

THIRD ROUTE

⑲ **Affaitati Palace - Civic Museum and National Art Gallery** - *Via Manzoni*

⑳ **St. Luke Church** - *Viale Trento e Trieste*

㉑ **Raimondi Palace** - *Corso Garibaldi*

㉒ **St. Agatha Church** - *Corso Garibaldi*

㉓ **St. Benedict** - *Via dei Mille*

5

SS. Margherita and Pelagia Church: *1. Second span of the nave: water springing forth from the rock; 2. Christ among the Doctors, by G. Campi; 3. Stanga-Rossi San Secondo Palace; 4. Via Trecchi leading to St. Agatha Church; 5. Courtyard of Trecchi Palace.*

95

Affaitati Palace

If we turn down via Solferino after leaving Piazza del Duomo we reach Piazza Roma where the old St.Dominic Church stood until 1869; there, in the big cloister attached to the church, used to meet the members of the Bakers' guild.

Along via Manzoni, which runs along the public gardens, rose once, in the second half of the 16th century, one of the most peculiar palaces of the 16th century in Cremona: Vidoni Palace, later called Archinto and finally Pagliari, a building which has been recently attributed to Francesco Dattaro, also called Pizzafuoco (? -1576).

Further on, at the beginning of the small Paolo Sarpi Square, we turn left to via Ugolani Dati. The name of the street refers to the last events which affected the Palace, originally belonging to the rich and noble Affaitati family. Marchese Gian Carlo Affaitati, to whom Pietro Aretino dedicated the fourth volume of his «Letters», began in 1561 the building of this aristocratic abode which was completed around 1570 by his son Francesco.

In the 18th century Marquess Magio initiated a series of changes in the interior, commissioning the work to architect Antonio Arrighi, the author of a spectacularly grand staircase built in 1769. Finally Marchionness Antonia Ugolani, the widow of Marquess Luigi Dati, left in 1826, according to a pompously rethorical inscription walled up on the top of the staircase, the Brothers of St.John of God as her only heirs; three years later the Brothers abandoned the old hospital devoted to the Blessed Crowned Virgin Mary and came to live in the palace. On 14 March 1838, «after the nearby houses had been demolished», architect Carlo Visioli began to build a new wing of the Palace

thus prolonging it up to the cross-roads of via Palestro. After the suppression of the Religious Order in 1866, a committee was assigned the administration of the Palace on behalf of the Town Council. In 1935, when even the hospital was suppressed, the Municipality turned the old aristocratic palace into the present seat of the Town Museum and of the Government Library.

1. Affaitati Palace, seat of the Municipal Museum, the Government Library and the Art Gallery; 2. Museum: Roman composite capital in Parian marble with lions; 3. Museum: fragment of a mosaic (12th century); 4. Staircase leading into the halls.

The calm harmony of this façade, which is divided horizontally and shows only pilaster-strips in its middle and at the two extreme ends, w.s made solemn by classically decorated windows, similar to aedicules, having alternatively triangular or round tympana. So, the 16th century palace gradually took on solemn features and was enlarged longitudinally; at the same time relevant plastic decorations were concentrated only in some areas. In the Affaitati Palace architect Francesco Dattaro was able to reinterpret with a more modern style the 15th century Raimondi Palace,

1

2

a regular brickwork cube which represented a suitable abode for a refined humanist. This palace of the 16th century, on the contrary, was not anymore the home of a merchant's or a banker's family but the residence of a small court gathered around the members of a family which had suddendly become famous and powerful through a princely dignity or some other titles of nobility.

Inside the building the ornamental panels over the doors of some halls on the piano nobile — noble floor — (now offices belonging to the library) are of particular interest; they were painted by Giacomo Guerrini (1718-1793) and represent **the mythological tale of Cupid and Psyche**.

In front of the entrance to the Government Library is the Ala Ponzone Town Museum. Its name refers to the munificent will of Marquess Ala Ponzone who donated his collection in 1842 for the benefit of scholars and artists in Cremona. The present Town Museum, recently enriched by significant donations, was set up forty years later by joining the wealth of the Ala Ponzone collection

3

Municipal Museum: *1. The Virgin on the throne and worshipper, by B. Bembo; 2. St. Filippo in the style of Bramante (Pietro Ispano); 3. Ceiling tablet by Bonifacio Bembo; 4. Eternal Father, by C. Boccaccino; 5. Decapitation of the Baptist, by A. Campi; 6. Virgin Mary's Assumption, by B. Campi, detail.*

4

5

6

to the one preserved in the Provincial Museum, founded in 1867.

The picture gallery, which is now being restructured, preserves in its 24 rooms a remarkable and interesting survey of the Cremonese Art of which we can only mention the most outstanding names: *14th-15th centuries*: Bonifacio and Benedetto Bembo; *16th century*: Boccaccio and Camillo Boccaccino; Gian Francesco Bembo and Altobello Melone; Giulio, Antonio, Bernardino and Vincenzo Campi; Bernardino Gatti; Sofonisba Anguissola and Giovanni Battista Trotti; *17th-18th centuries*: Luigi Miradori, Angelo Innocente Massarotti, Agostino Bonisoli, Sigismondo Francesco Boccaccino and Giovanni Angelo Borroni; *19th century*: Giuseppe Diotti, Giovanni Carnovali, also called Piccio, and a number of works by Cremonese artists who were born and active between the end of the 19th and the first half of the 20th century.

Municipal Museum: *1. Madonna on the throne with Child, St. Giovannino and St. Nicolò, by G.F. Bembo; 2. St. Thomas's incredulity, a sketch on drawing paper made by G. Diotti for the Cathedral fresco; 3. Giovanni Carnovali, also called Piccio: a portrait.*

3

Municipal Museum:
1. G. Gaspare
Pedone: harp; 2.
G.C. Procaccini: The
Guardian Angel; 3.
G.P. da Rho: St.
Anthony Abbot (a
bas-relief); 4.
Illuminated Choir-
book by Lorenzo
Fodri: Tobiah the
Old.

St. Luke Church

Walking along the Neoclassical extension of Affaitati Palace we reach via Palestro; then we turn right and go on until we cross via Trento Trieste. After about a 200 metres' walk we enter the secluded, small square of St.Luke, still retaining the same old cobbled paving which has been almost completely removed from the streets of Cremona.

Close to the simple saddle façade, with a graceful 15th century prothyrum, is a small, simple, octagonal temple devoted to the Resurrected Christ, built in 1503 to protect a revered image of the Saviour, frescoed on the left buttress of the façade, from the ravages of time and as a votive offering for the deliverance from the plague which threatened the town in 1502.

Towards the end of the 18th century the historiographer T.A.Variani from Cremona drew up a list of the ancient inscriptions preserved in the town and mentioned among others a memorial stone which testifies that the foundation stone of St.Luke Church was laid by Cardinal Marco Oddone on 21 September 1165. Moreover the same stone reveals that the Cardinal himself had made rich donations for the construction of the church and this is perhaps why he chose, two years later, to be buried in St.Luke's.

The present church, however, most probably results from an enlargement of the first temple, if we are to trust an inscription carved on the second pilaster from the left-hand side which reports that: «these columns were raised in the days of brother Giroldo, administrator of this building, in 1272». So, almost one century had allegedly passed from the foundation of the church to the building of the columns, and indeed it is too long a time for a small church. The graceful façade, divided by four marked buttresses which lend rhythm to the smooth brickwork surface, is today at a slightly lower level than the original one both because the «parvis» has been raised and also because of a renovation carried out by Andrea Pisenati in 1471. About sixty years earlier the rich merchant Aghinorio Aqualonga, living in the parish of St.Luke, had the entrance portal decorated with an elegant prothyrum and had commissioned a sacristy and his family's chapel inside the church.

1

All these events relating to the construction are still evident on the façade, namely in the two Gothic windows, in the framings of two faded frescoes dated from the late 17th century on the central buttresses, in the harmonious terracotta decoration of the rose-window, in the small intertwined pointed arches along the eaves cornice and perhaps in the two small lateral rose-windows, which are now walled up. These changes are still more evident in the interior, although the Barnabites commissioned to architect Arborio Mella from Vercelli radical restructuring works when, after the invalidation of the Napoleonic suppressions of Orders, they were readmitted in Cremona in 1881 by Bishop Geremia Bonomelli. Moreover, a recent restoration carried out in 1977 wiped out a conventional Neo-Gothic decoration by the painter Costa from Vercelli because it covered the exposed brick surface which is thought to have been the original wall arrangement.

The interior of the church, although retaining an atmosphere of deep and collected silence, typical of the Romanesque buildings, appears barren due to the lock of works of art, while documents dating back to the 18th century mention a significant quantity of them. A plausible explanation for this can be found in the different Religious Orders which alternatively governed the church during the centuries: in fact it was assigned to the secular clergy from its origins to 1528; then to the Amadeiti Friars of Observance and, after they were joined to the Friars Minor by the Pope St.Pius V in 1567, the pastoral care of the church remained in the hands of the latter until 1772. At the end of the 18th century St.Luke became again a parish for secular priests; it was turned into an auxiliary church of St.Agatha church in 1817 and it was later governed by the Capuchin friars and, finally, in 1881, by the Regular Clergy of St.Paul, commonly known as Barnabites.

At the entrance of the sacristy which lies at the end of the small right aisle is a picture by Giacomo Guerrini (1718-1793) representing **the Barnabite Father Alessandro Sauli on his knees before St.Paul**. In this valuable work, signed and dated 17(5)8 and mentioned for the first time in the Artistic-historical guide by Luigi Corsi (1819),

2

3

Guerrini seems to be clearly oriented towards a more luminous painting than the dramatic and violent one of his first works characterized by marked contrasts of light-and-shade. The colouring is in fact based upon a use of light and shade which is typically Venetian and no longer so vibrating as in the works by Caravaggio.

The present sacristy is arbitrarily divided into two parts and it is therefore impossible to understand the original position of the sacristy and of

1. St. Luke Church; 2. Columniferous lion of the Prothyrum; 3. Nave column: 15th-century frescoes, detail.

the attached *Aghinori Chapel*, both erected in 1419 for the rich merchant Aghinorio Aqualonga and frescoed by Antonino De Ferraris. The first room still contains fragments of **episodes from the life of St.John the Baptist** and, on the vault, **the four Evangelists**; on the vault of the second room are the **Doctors of the Church** and, on the walls, **the Annunciation** and **the contrast between the three living and the three dead persons**. In spite of the date of these works, the evident Lombard influence of the International Gothic style clearly shows, particularly in the last two frescoes, a taste for profane and realistic details in religious themes and even macabre memories of the Medieval culture.

Back to the small square, before going down Garibaldi Avenue and reaching then St.Agatha Church, it is advisable to stop a while in front of the *small temple of Christ Resurrected*, which, according to a recent suggestion, is ascribable to architect Bernardino De Lera, the closest to Bartolomeo Gadio among his successors and followers. De Lera, who interpreted the example of structural logics and of strict spatial unity laid down by Gadio by giving more importance to the gracefulness of the ensemble, was able to create a beautifully harmonious masterpiece in which the different decorative elements are indeed all governed by a rigorous spatial unity.

In the interior, for which is not easy to be granted a visit, Giovanni Battista Trotti, also called Malosso (1556-1619), frescoed the cupola and painted on canvas episodes from the life of Christ: **the Nativity, the Prayer in the garden of Gethsemane, the ascent to Calvary** and **the Crucifixion** on the surfaces among the pilaster-strips; on the panels over the doors **the Circumcision, the Flagellation and Jesus nailed to the cross**. Malosso gave here particular emphasis to a colouring preciousness in which he stressed naturalistic particulars and made even the shadows transparent.

Raimondi Palace

The present Milan Gate was called St.Luke Gate until 1293, because it rose near the old church. In 1793 the Gate was rebuilt by architect Faustino Rodi and renovated again in 1826. Finally, in 1902, it was demolished to leave room for the present large square.

At the beginning of Garibaldi Avenue, on the left side, is the 18th century façade of Stanga - Rossi St.Secondo Palace which however no longer possesses its beautiful portal, one of the most significant 15th century works sculptured by Gio-

3

4

5

vanni Pietro and Gabriele from Rho, Pietro from Vimercate and Daniele Castello; the portal was first sold to a private buyer and then, in 1875, to the Louvre Museum.

Not far from here, on the right, Raimondi Palace stands in all its geometrical elegance and refinement. According to two marble panels sculptured inside the pilaster-strips of its simple portal, Eliseo Raimondi was not only the owner of the palace, but also the one who planned it. This refined humanist is mentioned by a document dated 1511 as a «building expert»; nevertheless the most reliable hypothesis suggests the name of architect Bernardino De Lera as the artist who, perhaps influenced by the ambitions of his client, planned the whole building at the construction of which worked collaborators like Giovanni Pietro from Rho and Gaspare Pedone. As for the date, 1496, visible on the façade, it probably refers to the completion of the front and the courtyard, which, although unfortunately restructured in the last

century, can be ideally reconstructed thanks to a detailed description dated 1786.

On the clear and calm façade, in the traditional division into two floors on which coupled pilaster strips run, the stone ashlars, polished and arranged in pleasant rows, give the whole Palace an unusual and graceful lightness. Nothing here is heavy, not even on the ground floor where slender, flat pilaster-strips, alternated with square windows framed by elegant hood-moulds, start from a low bench-socle. Above is the sweet projection of the cornice whose soft and gentle shadow does not darken the Palace's front but envelops it with a plastic effect.

1. An old postcard showing the portal of Palazzo Stanga-Rossi S. Secondo (now in the Louvre Museum); a copy of the portal can be seen in the Council Hall in Palazzo Comunale.
2. Monumental room in Palazzo Stanga.
3. Palazzo Raimondi, seat of the International School of Violinmaking.
4-5. Façade and courtyard of Palazzo Stanga of Palestro.

St. Agatha Church

Past Raimondi Palace and continuing towards the centre of the town, Garibaldi Avenue becomes larger, reaching the size of a small square near Cittanova Palace and St.Agatha Church which stand with similar importance in front of one another.

The sober and imposing façade of the Town Hall of the «Città Nova» and the neoclassical front of the church brings us back to the time when the old town, still within the boundaries of its walls, corresponding approximately to the old Roman camp, was beginning to spread towards the countryside where the so-called «borghi» (suburbs) had already sprung up.

The first original document giving information about St.Agatha Church, «lying outside the town of Cremona, not far from Pertuso Gate», dates back to 26 September 1086. The same is reported by the church's foundation act (1077), while the «borgo» of «Città Nova» is mentioned by a notarial act dated 2 May 1124. It is not easy to give evidence of whether a previous church stood on the place where the present one stands, even if some local historiographers speak of a sacred building datable back to the 6th century. Therefore the oldest date related to St.Agatha is still 1077, although it has been copied from the Sicardo Codex (1210), and refers to a donation of three plots of land and a church by a married couple, Pietro and Cristina, and their relatives to Pope Gregory VII. The temple mentioned by the donation was devoted to St.Agatha and governed by

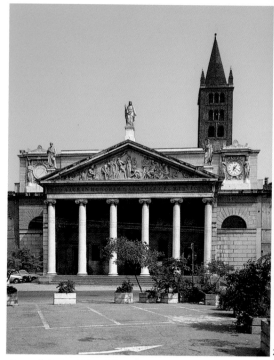

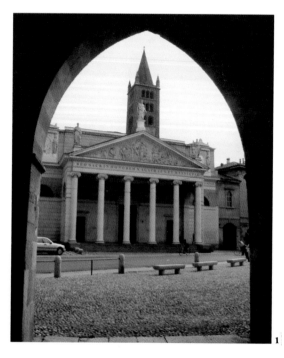

regular clergy until 1090; then it was assigned to the Regular Canons of the Congregation of St.Mary Fregionaia who held it until 1454. Then, after the death of Parish Priest Bono Uspinelli, the church was assigned to four Commendators the last of whom, secretary of Pope Pius II, succeeded in 1564 in turning St.Agatha Church into a secular parish church outside the jurisdiction of the Bishop of Cremona. However the days of its highest splendour were during the 12th and 13th centuries, when the flourishing commercial centre of the «Città Nova», although lying within the new walls of the City State (1169-1177), did not want to lose its self-government and, proudly opposing the Ghibelline noblemen of the town, raised Cittanova Palace in 1256. This significant example of civil architecture of the 13th century risked to be demolished in order to leave room for a conventional monument to Giuseppe Garibaldi, a work by the sculptor Andrea Malfatti (1886) from Trent.

Like the Cathedral and the Town Hall, St.Agatha Church and Cittanova Palace were therefore also an example of the relationship existing between Papacy and Empire, Guelphs and Ghibellines, a relationship which sometimes turned to intense struggles.

When Frederick «Barbarossa», who had been heavily defeated in Legnano some months earlier by the Lombard League — in which Cremona also participated, although belatedly — came to the town to regain its support, he was lodged in a house belonging to St.Agatha Church. On that occasion he solemnly swore not to cause any damage to the town and its territory, not to declare war and to help Cremona against the threats of the neighbouring Lombard towns. A memorial stone dated 1177 was discovered in 1965 in St.Agatha Church in which a building, perhaps the bell-tower, is mentioned and whose construction dates back to the time of the agreements between Barbarossa and Pope Alexander III. The stone is now walled up above the socle of the left transept wall.

Archive documents and the surviving architectonic elements of the church — the bell-tower and fragments of a mosaic floor preserved in the Town Museum — are not sufficient to suggest any datings earlier than the year 1200. Particularly interesting for the architectonic history of the church is the discovery, made in 1755, of mosaic fragments found in the presbitery, «six ells» below the floor. It is therefore to be assumed that the primitive church had a crypt and the finding represents what has remained of the old Romanesque floor.

It was not until about thirty years later (1496) that St.Agatha, turned into a secular parish church, was radically restructured according to a project by Bernardino De Lera, carried out by the master masons Pietro and Matteo da Prato. The church was rebuilt with one nave and four aisles and the old saddle façade, with its small rose-window and the two cuspidal towers at both sides as it appears in a tarsia by Plàtina (1455-1500), was replaced by the smooth and geometrical surfaces typical of Bernardino De Lera's style. In 1598 it was «prettily embellished» by paintings whose traces were still visible at the beginning of the 19th century, when architect Luigi Voghera began the new façade in 1839 giving it the appearance of a Greek temple.

When the restructuring was completed (first decade of the 16th century), the painter Bernardino Ricca frescoed in 1510 the vault with «**intertwined plants and several Putti**», as is reported by guides published in Cremona between the 18th and the 19th centuries. But unfortunately these precious remains of a glorious past were also wiped out, covered by a uniform lime colour. Only towards the end of the century (1872-1873) Giovanni Bergamaschi (1828-1903) frescoed, in the middle of three spans, **the Allegories of Faith, Hope and Charity**, while the ornaments with light-and-shadow effects were carried out by Aurelio Pucci.

Inside the church, close to the right wall is the *Mausoleum of Pietro Francesco Trecchi*, built between 1502 and 1505 for the altar devoted to St.Jerome in St.Vincent Church, as Marquess Trec-

3

chi himself had ordered to his brother Giacomo in the testament drawn up on 16 May 1502. The sarcophagus was moved to St.Agatha in 1789 and, after several replacements in different parts of the church, was placed into its present position. Scholars have agreed since long time to attribute the project of the mausoleum to Gian Cristoforo Romano (1470-1512) while a very recent hypothesis has suggested that Giovanni Gaspare Pedone may be the one who actually carried out the work.

Past the altars devoted to St.Sebastian and to the SS.Relics, we come to St.Agatha chapel with its vault frescoed by Angelo Innocente Massarotti (1654-1723). This altar jealously preserves *the Holy Panel*, a much valuable work painted on both sides by an anonymous painter from Northern Italy, active towards the end of the 13th century. On one side the Panel tells, in four parallel bands, episodes from the martyrdom of the Saint woman: **the temptation of Aphrodisia who tries to persuade Agatha to yield to Praetor Quintianus; the Saint woman before Quintianus; the flagellation; the breast's extirpation; St.Peter visiting the martyr in prison; Agatha on burning coals; Catania struck by an earthquake and the prayer of the Saint woman; the dead Agatha is surrounded by angels, one of whom places the Holy Panel under the Saint woman's head; Quintianus drowns in the Simeto river.**

On the opposite side are **the Virgin with the Child** in her arms and, above an indented arch, **the Descent of the Holy Ghost** on Pentecost morning.

---

1. Cittanova Palace and St. Agatha Church; 2. St. Agatha Church; 3. Mausoleum of Pietro Francesco Trecchi.

109

Much has been written about the anonymous and yet great author of the panel and the critics, although recognizing influences from Tuscany, Veneto and Emilia, agree to attribute the masterpiece to a good painter from Lombardy. Roberto Longhi makes a comparison between the «Master of the Panel of St.Agatha» and the initiator of Italian painting Cenni di Pepo, commonly known as Cimabue, and calls the former «the Cimabue of Northern Italy».

Beside the entrance door to the bell-tower is a canvas which, although having little artistic value is of some historical interest. The painting, dated 1634 and representing **the intercession of the Purgatory souls**, belonged to the Confraternity of the «Sacred Conception of the Blessed Virgin», found-

ed in the collegiate church of St.Agatha by father Matteo Cappuccino on 14 March 1610. The altar in front of which the priest is celebrating shows a perfect reproduction of the imposing gilded altar-piece (1587) of the left aisle, on which previously an image of the Virgin was frescoed which perhaps corresponds to the one which is now in the attic over the entablature of the altar-piece itself.

To the right of the presbitery is a small chapel decorated with two canvases, the former representing **the Martyrdom of St.Stephen**, a work by Giovanni Battista Trotti, also called Malosso (1556-1619), the latter, attributable to the school of Giovanni Angelo Borroni (1684-1772), representing **several Saints in Heaven's Glory**. The most interesting aspect, however, is that the Saints represented in the canvas are those to whom many of the Cremonese churches still existing in the 18th century were devoted.

Now we come into the presbitery which is now excessively long because of the demolition of the

---

St. Agatha's: *1. The Sacred Panel, painted on both sides by an unknown painter from 13th century. The front narrates the story of the Saint's martyrdom; 3. The Holy Family and St. Mary Magdalene, by Boccaccio Boccaccino.*

old apse shamefully carried out at the beginning of our century. On the wide walls, divided by a frescoed false pilaster-strip, Giulio Campi (c.1505-1573) painted four episodes from the martyrdom of St.Agatha: **The breast extirpation; St.Peter visiting the Martyr in prison; the Saint woman condemned to the fire torture; the funeral of the Saint woman.** The thirty-year-old painter from Cremona was able to absorb every stylistic suggestion without being an imitator: on the contrary, he mingled the different styles with an enormous sense of human understanding, that is to say he could remain true to a deep spontaneity and to an original poetry.

In the middle of the apse, inside a carved and gilded altar-piece, commissioned in 1902 to the Cremonese artist Adolfo Guindani, is a panel by Gervasio Gatti (1550-1630) representing **St.Agatha before praetor Quintianus**. The work, signed and dated 1608, gives emphasis to conventional arrangements, to solemn and measured gestures, almost artificial and devoid of feelings, and to opaque colours, all elements giving the scene a mannered grandiosity.

In the left transept and namely in the small chapel corresponding to the one devoted to the Blessed Sacrament is a panel representing **the Holy Family and St.Mary Magdalene** recently attributed to Boccaccio Boccaccino (c.1466-1525) after a restoration (1980) which has proved the signature «Galeazius Campus» to be a fake and has made the two last digits of the date, 1518, visible. Originally the panel was in St.Luke Church, but its presence in St.Agatha Church was mentioned by local scholars in 1858. Boccaccino, brought up in

the cultural environment of Ferrara, left soon the court of the Este family to develop a sweeter style following the dreaming poetry of Perugino but he was also influenced by the pictorial lyricism of Bellini.

In front of the door which leads into the sacristy is the lugubrious *monument of Giovanni Battista Stanga* and his wife *Costanza Meli*, sculptured in 1538 for St.Vincent Church by a certain Vincenzo Lanfranco.

The two paintings representing **St.Catherine of Alexandria and St.Cecilia**, which hang at both sides of the Stanga mausoleum have been recently attributed to the Cremonese painter Gabriele Zocchi (1601-1660) who lived at the parish of St.Agatha and whose dates of birth and death are given here for the first time.

Finally, over the high altar is a big canvas representing **the Miracle of the loaves**, painted by the little known Marc'Antonio Ghislina (1676-1756) from Casale Monferrato. On both sides of the same entrance door are two valuable pictures by Bernardino Campi (1522-1591), one of the most prolific Cremonese painters of the 16th century. It is clearly recognizable that, when he was pressed by his clients to produce more and therefore not concentrated enough, he yielded to the «Mannerism» he had learned from the great Emilian masters and by the brothers Campi, his fellow-citizens.

St. Agatha: *1. Story of St. Agatha's life, by G. Campi; 2. St. Benedict: ceiling painted in fresco by A. Massarotti, detail.*

The Monastery of St. Benedict

A few steps beyond St.Hilarius Church, a wide and irregular group of buildings called «Ex-caserme» (ex-barracks) is enclosed by via Dei Mille, via Stretta Lunga, via Giovanni Carnevali, via Racchetta and via Chiara Novella. Of all these street names only the last one reminds us of the centuries-old, troubled history of one of the biggest town monasteries ever built in those suburban areas called for the first time in 1163 «in clausis in braida», i.e. cultivated land outside the walls. In fact, a narrow street near St.Augustine Church still retains the name of via Breda, a name derived from the old «Braida». This large belt which encircled Cremona became part of the town itself between 1169 and 1177 when the second town walls were built. However, the information about the foundation of the first monastery devoted to the SS.Sylvester and Benedict refer to a century earlier, namely to 1 October 1089 when Abbot Damiano of Nonantola authorized the building of the said monastery assigning to it a plot of land «near the town». Local historians do not completely agree on the date and different hypotheses have been suggested. Some believe that, after the foundation, the Benedictines remained there until 1069 and that they left this part of town because of the plague and other calamities; others say that the Monastery of St.Benedict was erected in 1064 thanks to the devout will of Ardingo and Edina, a married couple. One thing, in any way, is undoubted: the first monks of the monastery were followed by the Benedictine nuns, although in a document dated 9 September 1100 the presence of monks is still mentioned. Oberto, Bishop of Cremona, in order to put an end to the sharing of the same monastery by the two different groups, assigned in 1153 the church and the attached cloister to Abbess Giuliana on condition that she acknowledge the episcopal jurisdiction. After a short period during which no cloistered-nuns lived in the monastery the Benedictine nuns of St.Mary of Fontanelle returned to St.Benedict in 1260. From then onwards other religious orders and consequent changes of jurisdiction followed one another in the monastery until, in 1591, Pope Gregory XIV, from Cremona, put it definitively under the authority of the Bishop of the town. The last event of St.Benedict's centuries-old history dates back to 1784, when Emperor Joseph II suppressed it in order to establish a new seat for the College of the Canonesses of St.Charles (1786-1798).

The cloister of St.Clare was added in the first decades of the 14th century to St.Benedict.

A document recording a privilege of Bishop

2

Omobono Madalberti dated 1233 reports that the convents of St.Francis and St.Damiano, in which nuns lived, rose then in the so-called «chiusi», i.e. «outside St.Luke Gate». The convent of St.Damiano was later assigned to the Poor Clares order who soon became increasingly numerous. Wars forced the Poor Clares, as had happened with the first St.Benedict monks, to move to somewhere else inside the town walls, namely to the parish of St.Paul, beside the Monastery of St.Benedict, and consequently to build, in 1330, a new Convent which they devoted to St.Clare and which soon became the object of privileges and donations.

The last monastery, the Monastery of the «Corpus Domini» - also called «Corpo di Cristo» by documents, the Italian translation of its Latin name - originated thanks to the firm will of duchess Bianca Maria Visconti who obtained by Pope Callisto III the permission to build a new Convent for the daughters of Cremonese noblemen. The devout duchess made available to the order a palace of her property which stood near St.Benedict and St.Clare and perhaps because of the short distance the original denomination of «Christ's Body» was changed into «Chiara Novella». The three groups of buildings, although passing through different events, remained almost untouched until the ruinous Habsburg suppressions.

In fact in 1782 the Monasteries of St.Clare and of the «Corpus Domini» were suppressed and two years later the same fate struck St.Benedict.

Particularly interesting, beside the beautiful internal cloisters which are almost impossible to visit, is **the glory of the Benedictine order**, frescoed by Angelo Innocente Massarotti (1654-1723) on the vault of the external church of the former Monastery of St.Benedict. A restoration carried out in 1986 saved from gradual decay this work which had such a strong importance for the Cremonese Baroque culture and emphasized both its great perspective effects and the dramatic gestures of its characters, made still livelier by means of a colouring typical of the 17th century. During the presentation of the restored work to the citizens of Cremona the friendly relationship between Massarotti and the Benedictine nuns was mentioned to suggest plausible hypotheses about the dating of the fresco. The document recording the death of the painter, who was then living at the Parish of SS. Vincent and James, gives, however, a different hint: although the artist is mentioned here as «benefactor of our church», i.e. of St.Vincent, his last will was to be buried in the external church of the Poor Clares of «Corpus Domini». So, it was not near the Benedictine nuns that this talented interpreter of 17th century art in Cremona asked to be put to rest after a very intense and active life.

Episcopal Seminary: The Berenzi Museum

When Monsignor Geremia Bonomelli (1831-1914), appointed Bishop of Cremona by Pius IX in 1871, came to his new Diocese, he found it in a very poor state. The Seminary had only 32 pupils and many of them had to be expelled before the end of the school term because

of their theological mistakes. The clergy of the seminary, which had been reduced in number, amounted to 35 apostates and to many priests coming from different Dioceses, and some of them had embraced the most extremist and subversive patriotic ideas. Bishop Bonomelli initiated then a reformation of the clergy, discussed and approved by the 1880 Synod, and pursued it zealously, or indeed, as he himself said, with «excess of zeal». The pastoral activity ended in the building of the Seminary. Before 1872, in fact, seminarists had lived at boarding houses or, anyway, outside the Seminary, where they only attended lessons. The predecessor of Bishop Bonomelli, Monsignor Antonio Novasconi, had closed for financial difficulties the small Seminary devoted to St.Charles and had gathered the pupils into the big Seminary near St.Margherita Church. The controversy arisen between the Bishop and the State Property Office about the proprietorship of St.Charles Seminary and the existing difficulties in enlarging the Seminary of St.Margherita persuaded Monsignor Bonomelli to sell both Seminaries and to buy a large building outside the town in a place called Angel's. The expensive enterprise was completed two years later, in 1887, using «only the means supplied by the Diocese». A circular letter is still preserved in which the Bishop congratulates on the successful outcome of the works.

Among the various activities to which Monsignor Bonomelli devoted himself, particular atten-

tion must be paid to his constant care for the artistic wealth of the Diocese. The first assembly of the Diocesan Committee for Sacred Art, for example, was held on 31 January 1906 and the idea of Monsignor Angelo Berenzi to set up a Museum for the Seminary, later called after him, goes back perhaps to that event. Inaugurated in 1913 and devoted to the memory of Berenzi's mother Caterina Gorno, who died that same year, the Museum preserves, according to the testimony of its founder, «material which I have collected since my childhood and then bought in different parts of the world over a period of fifty years...»; «...be-

side the various collections of bronze and terracotta objects from excavations, of weapons, coins, medals, chinaware, earthenware, enamels, miniatures and carved objects of ivory, tortoiseshell and semi-precious stone, there are also etchings by Rembrandt, Durer, Callot and Morghen; paintings by Romanino, Parmigianino, Mazzolino, Cima da Conegliano, Campi, Gatti, Chiaveghino and Diotti; studies by Carnevali (Piccio) and works by Bertesi: as for modern art, there are paintings and sculptures by Lodovico Pogliaghi, Vespasiano Bignami, Antonio Rizzi, Colombi, Sibellato, Minozzi, Biazzi, Rescalli, Romolo del Bò, Domenico Trentacoste, Monti, Ferraroni, Sgarbi and many others». Although the collection does not always respond to an enlightened taste and still needs a more careful critical analysis, some of its works form nevertheless an artistic wealth of significant importance. Among these works are: *the Nativity* by Altobello Melone; *three floor panels* by Bonifacio Bembo; *the Depo-*

1. Palace of the Episcopal Seminary; 2. Berenzi Museum: Nativity, by Altobello Melone; 3. Berenzi Museum: St. Carlo's birth, by Genovesino.

sition from the Cross by Dionigi Calvert; *a portrait* by Bartolomeo Passarotti; *two episodes from the life of St.Charles* by Luigi Miradori, also called Genovesino; *the mystic marriage of St.Catherine* by Gervasio Gatti; *the Holy Family* by Angelo Innocente Massarotti; *an oldman's head* by Pietro Martire Neri; four *episodes from the Bible* attributable to the painter Pasquale Ottino from Verona; *Magdalene* by Regnier; *Christ resurrected*, a wooden sculpture by Giacomo Bertesi and *Judas kiss* (a fragment) by Giuseppe Diotti.

St. Sigismund Church

At the time of the marriage between Duke Francesco Sforza and Bianca Maria Visconti the small St.Sigismund Church, governed by the monks of Vallombrosa, must have really been standing in the countryside. In fact the present temple, erected for the devout Duchess twenty years later and on the same place, in memory of that happy event, can still be seen at the farthest outskirts of the town on the road which leads to Casalmaggiore. The origins and the denomination of the

primitive place of worship devoted to St.Mary and the Apostles Philip and James are lost in legend, although they are mentioned by a document dated 1153. What is undoubted is that the dedication to St.Sigismund, wanted by the monks of Vallombrosa, followed their settling in the church and the attached monastery about one century later.

This small monastery would certainly have been forgotten if, on 25 October 1441, during the feast of SS.Crisante and Daria, the marriage of Francesco Sforza and Bianca Maria Visconti, the daughter of the Duke of Milan, Filippo Maria, had not been celebrated there. By bringing as a dowry the town and its territory the bride justified the constant attention which she will later on pay to Cremona, its artists, convents and churches. Let us mention here for example the Monastery of Corpus Domini, and the altar devoted to SS.Crisante and Daria in St.Augustine Church on both sides of which, as mentioned above, Bonifacio Bembo had portrayed the noble married couple in a devout attitude. In order to build the new church and a larger monastery, thus replacing the two crumbling buildings and, at the same time, remembering the marriage celebrated twenty years earlier, Duchess Bianca Maria obtained in 1461 by Pius II the suppression of the Community of the Vallombrosa monks which were replaced by the Hieronymites, a recently established Spanish congregation which the Duchess herself contributed in introducing in Lombardy. The foundation stone was solemnly laid on 20 June 1463 and after its finding, occurred in 1710 during the construction of the new altar, it was placed behind the altar where it is still visible.

Works started with alacrity but were stopped almost suddenly after the death of Francesco Sforza, in 1466, and of Duchess Bianca Maria in 1468. From then on, mainly for financial reasons, the building activity went on very slowly. In fact, it was not until 1475 that Gian Galeazzo, succeeded to Francesco Sforza, confirmed to the church its ducal privileges and its exemption, so that in 1480 the Hieronymite monks were allowed to open a tavern in Farisengo. Works were resumed with eagerness under Ludovico Sforza who, in 1485, beside the usual annuities, granted 500 ducats to the Monastery, and in 1487 made available for the Fabric 4200 ducats more each year until works were completed. This is mentioned by a document dated 1482 reporting the fact that a bequest for a chapel in St.Sigismund's was left during that very year. A further confirmation

St. Sigismund Church.

comes from *two* slender *glass ampullae* and by *a thick brick* (now in the first chapel to the right) found in 1963 in the foundations of the façade when urgent works for the strengthening of the façade itself were carried out. The date engraved on the brick, 31 August 1492, marks the beginning of the building of the façade and the two ampullae, containing wine and oil, represented an auspicious symbol for the initiated works which, however, would be the last act of the architectural history of the monumental group of buildings.

The local historiographers agree to attribute the plan and the carrying out of St.Sigismund's to Bartolomeo Gadio, appointed Commissioner general of the Milan Dukedom, who therefore was charged with official tasks and received recognitions by Francesco Sforza in the years 1451-1455.

It is worth mentioning a charming hypothesis according to which Averlino Antonio, also called Filarete (c.1400-1469), who was in Cremona in 1451 and in 1465, collaborated, at least in the first stage of the planning, with Gadio. To the name of the Florentine architect, who was asked to plan the «Sforziade» in Milan, i.e. a new urbanistic arrangement, should also be added the one of Aristotele Fioravanti from Bologna. Filarete brought into Lombardy the rational spatiality of Brunelleschi which, because of the red and white marble, took on a more common outline but also a more varied colouring. The involvement of Filarete and Fioravanti would explain the new architectonic sensibility, easily recognizable in St.Sigismund's marked apse structure and in the massive form of the quadrangular lantern. These

solutions by Gadio were remarkably far from the slender Gothic verticality which seemed then more usual in the Lombard architecture. Looking from outside at such a compact block of mass, marked by the sharp projections of the angular buttresses and crowned by a lowered lantern, which looks as suspicious as a watch tower, it is perhaps easier to understand the difference between the initial architectonic solution and the ones chosen for the longitudinal development of the nave and for the façade. The hypothetical central plan of the original church suggested by some scholars is therefore a reasonable suppposition. Moreover the death of Bartolomeo Gadio between 1483 and 1486 made the intervention of other architects necessary and the most quoted names are those of Guglielmo and Bernardino De Lera, considered as the best interpreters of Gadio's spatial vision. In addition, Bernardino, the author of the most prestigious buildings in Cremona towards the end of the 15th century, is also considered the author of the sober façade in which *the portal*, sculptured in 1578 by Sebastiano Nani (? -1587), perhaps according to a project by architect Giuseppe Dattaro (1540-1619), represents a striking note.

After entering this place which is really a very rich gallery of local paintings, particularly of the

St. Sigismund's: *1. Church interior; 2. Apsidal bowl-shaped vault: Christ in Glory and the Evangelists, fresco by B. Boccaccino.*

16th century, visitors will not be at once aware of the way St. Sigismund Church looked like when its essential structure was completed. Its architecture was then clearly and rationally designed by pilaster-strips, cornices and brickwork entablatures which delimited the bright plastered surfaces without decorations. Such an arrangement of pure structural logic carried out with sober elegance remained unchanged until 1520 when Altobello Melone frescoed the lowered cupola, re-painted in 1570 by Bernardino Campi (1522-1591).

The flourishing period for painting in St. Sigismund began in 1535 when Camillo Boccaccino (1504/5-1546) was commissioned a fresco on the bowl-shaped vault representing **Christ in his glory and the four Evangelists**. The theological and biblical connection linking the figures of the presbitery to those of the transept and the big nave's big vault have been acutely discovered and the parallels between Old and New Testament have been shown, all wanting to represent the only one theme: **Christ's glorification, prefigured in the killing of just Abel and in David beating Goliath and evoked by Isaac blessing Jacob as well as by a Jewish sacrifice, perhaps Melchizedek's**. These four small stories are painted by Boccaccino on the vault of the presbitery at both sides of **a glory of Angels supporting the cross**. Inside a very rich and refined decoration painted according to styles common in Rome and Mantua are **four very ele-**

gant Sybils which recall the figurative and chromatic dynamism of Correggio. All this was foreseen by the detailed commissioning document according to which clients were free to suggest the biblical episodes to be painted and painters in their turn were free to invent ornaments for the vault, the pilaster strips and the framings of the two windows. Finally, the portraits of the Dukes Francesco Sforza and Bianca Maria, of their son Galeazzo and their nephew Gian Galeazzo should have been painted on the entablature frieze. The agreement with Camillo Boccaccino for two frescoes in the presbitery, **Christ and the adulteress** and **the resurrection of Lazarus**, dates back to 1540. The formal elegance which even distorts the scene, the aristocratic outlines and the colour preciousness make of these evangelical episodes the most elaborate and typical of the Cremonese Mannerism of the 16th century. As for the figures painted with no pupils in their eyes, which usually make visitors disconcerted, no plausible hypothesis has been so far suggested and it is probable that the artist's oddity will remain unexplained. An in-

St. Sigismund's: *1.-2. Lazarus' resurrection, and Christ and the Adulteress, by B. Boccaccino; 3. Altar-piece on the High Altar, Madonna in Glory with the Saints Sigismund and Jerome, Crisante Daria with Francesco Sforza and Bianca Maria Visconti.*

3

1

2

teresting point is the stylistic change that Camillo Boccaccino was able to inscribe in his painting full of stylistic subtelties which came first from the culture of Rome, Venice and Mantua, and later from the works of Parmigianino.

While Camillo Boccaccino was displaying the imaginative excitement of his inspiration, the altarpiece for the high altar was commissioned to Giulio Campi (c.1505-1573) and a beautiful carved and gilded «ancona» to the carvers Paolo and Giuseppe Sacca, the latter continuing the work of his father after his death. Giulio Campi, who should have finished the work on the year following the signing of the agreement, actually completed it in 1539, as shown by the signature on the base of the column. The painter studied for

a long time the scene which would celebrate the patron saints Sigismund and Jerome, the Saints remembered every year on 25 October, Crisante and Daria, and the noble clients Francesco Sforza and Bianca Maria Visconti. In the upper part of the painting, in the middle of an Angelic glory, is a luminous apparition of the Virgin with Child.

The crowded group of people in the foreground, deeply absorbed in a luminescent languor, stands against the light and we get a glimpse of a landscape with almost vespertine hues, influenced by the stress on tonality typical of the style of Venice and Ferrara and contrasting with the flashing colours of the celestial vision of Emilian character.

The presbyterial Bench and **the Bench of the officiating priests**, valuable works by Giuseppe Sacca who painted the former in 1542 and the latter about twenty years later, have been recently moved against the walls of the presbitery.

If we want to keep to a chronological order two almost contemporary works are to be considered: the decoration of the transept wings and the frescoes of the first span of the vault. Giulio Campi, who had to finish the decoration within two years from the commission date, 1539, continued, according to the will of his clients, the learned theological parallelism begun some years earlier by Camillo Boccaccino. To **the Evangelists** on the bowl-shaped vault corresponded **four Prophets** on both sides of the big round window, and **four Doctors of the Latin Church** above the cornice, at the springer of the big arches. Camillo Boccaccino had frescoed **a group of Angels with the cross** in the middle of the vault, above the presbitery, and Giulio Campi painted a **glory of Angels bearing the instruments of Christ's passion**

in the middle of the transept's vault, inside octagonal frameworks. Finally to four episodes from the Old Testament painted by Boccaccino corresponded four more episodes equally referring to moments of Christ's life: **Solomon's judgement, the Queen of Sheba and King Solomon, the picking up of the manna and the water gushed out** of the rock. Campi represented in these frescoes the monumental and vibrating effects typical of the excited imagination by Pordenone, adding his own burning colouring.

During the intense activity of Campi for these paintings, Domenico De Siccis from Bologna, a totally unknown artist, was frescoing **Christ's resurrection and prophet Jonah expelled by the whale to the seashore** on the first span of the vault; **two Prophets** in the vaulting cells, **the monochromes and the frieze.** He was paid for the works on 9 August 1540 by his clients who, unsatisfied , dismissed him. Camillo Boccaccino and Giulio Campi, together with Bernardino Gatti and Bernardino Campi were assigned the work again.

Until then the decoration of the interior had been carried out according to a rigorous chrono-

St. Sigismund's: *1. Representation of the night, fresco by G. Campi; 2. Transept: Moses makes water spring forth from the rock, by G. Campi, detail; 3. Detail of the nave vault: the Tables of the Law, by G. Campi; 4.-5. Details of the transept arch by G. Campi; 6. Prophet Jonah by D. De Siccis.*

Mary and the Apostles Philip and James. One year before his death, in 1545, Camillo Boccaccino frescoed only **the Mysteries of the life of the Virgin** (1st chapel on the right, turning our back to the gate) and **two tondi** recently discovered behind the canvases by Gervasio Gatti, also called Soiaro (1550-1630). The flashing forms, the changing tonality and some realistic details (the banister, the roll window and the tray offered to the puerpera after the childbirth) close the first and most important chapter of the 16th century art in Cremona.

Bernardino Campi (1522-1591), frescoing the vault of the **chapel devoted to SS.Philip and James** (2nd chapel on the left turning one's back to the gate) follows the formal solutions of Boccaccino rendering them through a kind of jewelled colouring. Lamo, Campi's first biographer, reports that the painter wanted at all costs to have the so many paintings left by the artist in his workshop. In fact in 1560 Bernardino Campi had to decorate with putti and grotesques **the Mysteries of the life of the Virgin**, perhaps adding **the Adoration of the Magi**. The **two Prophets** in the big lunette over the altar-piece, **the Nativity** and **the Presentation of Mary to the temple**, frescoed in 1594 by Andrea Mainardi also called Chiaveghino (c.1550-1613/4), marked the definitive conclusion

logical, spatial and thematic order which will not be repeated anywhere in the temple. In fact the frescoes on the nave's vault are interrupted when the decoration of the first two chapels, devoted to the Virgin and to SS.Philip and James begins. The primitive small church governed by the monks of Vallombrosa, according to a testimony by Muratori, was in fact devoted to the Virgin

St. Sigismund's: *1.-2. Virgin Mary's birth and Virgin Mary's Presentation to the Temple. Medallions by Camillo Boccaccino; 3. The Ascension, by Bernardino Gatti; 4. St. Filippo's Chapel, vault frescoes by B. Campi.*

of a work which had started fifty years before. However, although Campi tried to keep to the formal theories of Boccaccino when carrying out his plans, he could never equal his unique art.

In 1549 the decoration of the second span was resumed with the big fresco representing the **Ascension** a work by Bernardino Gatti, also called Soiaro (c.1495-1576), while the remaining decoration of the vault was painted by Bernardino Campi. The parabolic arrangement of the clouds and of the angelic hosts, impending over the crowded group of Apostles, is broken by the bold, oblique cut of Christ who is ascending among the flashes of myriads of Angels, immaterial in the hot celestial light.

The remaining surfaces to be frescoed were the last span of the vault and the two areas on both sides of the round central rose-window. The work was commissioned completely to Giulio Campi who, between 1557 and 1559, painted **the episode of the Pentecost** in the middle of the ceiling, «opened» by an up-ward perspective, with very spectacular effects. The fresco by Campi, although recalling the bold solutions suggested by Camillo Boccaccino in the bowl-shaped vault, is nevertheless one of his most praised works and undoubtedly his masterpiece. Above the cornice, on both sides of the big, round window, are **the Archangel Gabriel** and **Our Lady of the Annunciation**. We should recall that the very same solu-

tion had been suggested by Campi for the counterfaçade of SS.Margherita and Pelagia Church.

When the work in the big vault, the transept, the presbitery and the apse was completed, the Hieronymite monks perhaps thought that the decoration painted in the cupola by Altobello Melone about forty years earlier was unsuitable for the church. However it was temporarily left as it was because they chose to decorate *the ten pilaster-strips* of the nave which were enlarged and supplied with new marble bases sculptured between 1563 and 1565 by the «picapreda» Sebastiano Nani. In the same period the brothers Giulio and Antonio Campi were paid for the gilding and the fresco decoration of the pilaster-strips in which they had to take into account the previous figurative example suggested by Camillo Boccaccino. With their vivid imagination the two brothers were able to mix rejoicing putti and animals, armours and musical instruments, flowers and fruits so as to create a unique interpretation of the classical «candelabra»-decoration of columns. Going back to the presbitery to admire the renovated cupola, frescoed in 1570 by Bernardino Campi, particular attention should be paid to **twenty-four figures in white stucco**, in various attitudes and arranged on both sides of each arch. The payments, carefully registered in the «Fabric Daybook» mention only Giulio Campi, while critics agree almost unanimously on recognizing above all the touch of Antonio, more interested in sculpture than his brother.

Past the monumental railings supported by a banister built by Angiolo Nani (? -1611) between 1592 and 1594, we come to the middle of the transept under the lowered cupola in which Bernardino Campi, summarizing the several themes of the elaborate iconographic plan, frescoed

Heaven, **populated by figures from the Old and the New Testament. The circular vision of the Eternal Father, surrounded by the heads of little Angels,** represents the ideal perspective point of the whole scene, winding up in groups and rhythmically divided by some standing figures in the foreground. Although the artist had taken into account the gradations of light and colours in relation to the strained forms and to the distance of the characters, his work does not reach the light and illusory boldness of Camillo Boccaccino and Giulio Campi. The very careful execution of the work, whose accuracy borders on virtuosity, did not go beyond a pleasant colouring having varied but always precious hues which are sometimes warm as gold and sometimes cold as silver.

Back into the nave, in order to try to have an

St. Sigismund's: *1. Vault of the nave. The Pentecost episode, a fresco by Giulio Campi; 2. Second Chapel on the left: altar-piece with the Saints Philip and Jacob, by G. Campi; 3. Transept dome: Paradise, a fresco by B. Campi.*

126

3

idea of the 16th century art in Cremona, it is first of all necessary to visit the chapels whose decoration dates back to the last thirty years of the 16th century. On the right is the already mentioned *chapel devoted to the Virgin* and in front of it, to the left, *the chapel devoted to St. Jerome*. Bernardino Campi, in 1566, painted only an altar-piece while Giovanni Battista Cambi, also called Bombarda, modelled richly decorated garlands and pompous frameworks for frescoes which were painted in 1625 by Camillo Gavassetti from Modena. Using refined lines and a careful descriptive skill Campi outlined the figures of **St. Jerome and St. Anthony Abbot** with such a harmony of formal beauty and expressive sincerity as to make it almost impossible to excel. In the following

chapel devoted to *SS. Apostles Philip and James* who, together with the Virgin, were the first Saints to whom the small church governed by the monks of Vallombrosa had been devoted, Bernardino Campi frescoed the vault in 1546 with **episodes from the life of the Apostle Philip** drawing them from an apocryphal book: «The Acts of Philip». The works for the renovation of the chapels were resumed in 1562 when an altar-piece with **two Saints set in a pleasant wooded surroundings** was commissioned to Giulio Campi. Payments for the work are mentioned by documents until 1568; from then on, when the concomitant commissions of works for St. Sigismund's demanded much of the enthusiastic painter's time, he rarely succeeded in honouring

127

the terms fixed by the agreements. On the walls are two large canvases representing **the martyrdom of St.James Minor and the miracle of the loaves**. The paintings bear the signature of Giulio Calvi, also called Coronaro, the titular organist of the church who, in 1591, was paid for two paintings sketched for him by the Cremonese Giovanni Battista Malosino. As Calvi died untimely the paintings were finished by Malosino, who was paid for them in 1596. All critics agree to recognize in the figure of Malosino instead of his nephew Euclide Trotti, the painter (1556-1619) who most probably commissioned in his turn the work to some pupil of his crowded workshop.

In front of this *chapel* is the one devoted to *St.John the Baptist*. All the works in this chapel, amid troubled events, lasted long and were carried out by Antonio Campi (1523-1587). Two years later the altar-piece representing **the Baptist's Beheading**, a work commissioned in 1563 while the artist was working with his brother Giulio at the decoration of the nave's pilasters, was only finished by two thirds so that it was replaced by another one which was paid in 1567. In the meantime Antonio Campi had finished the vault by modelling directly on the vaulting cells very elegant figures and elaborate frameworks which enclose **episodes from the life of the Baptist** painted with changing colours and with a refined, cameo-like drawing. It is believed that the altar-piece was slowly modified until 1579-80 when payments for the carving and gilding of the beautiful framework are recorded. The ideal of decoration pursued by Antonio and even more by his brother Giulio was suddenly abandoned in this work and in the following ones created by the younger artist who chose a more naturalistic path which evidently anticipates Caravaggio. From the dark fog of the prison a rogue springs upon the Baptist's body which is represented by means of an almost macabre realism. On one side is the lithe and provocative body of Salome, covered by a transparent veil, eagerly waiting for the Baptist's severed head painted with a pathetic realism. In 1577, when the altar-piece was almost finished, Campi painted and dated a fresco representing **the supper in the house of Simon the Pharisee**. In order to better enjoy the illusion of perspective of the painted architecture it is necessary to know that the point of view lies beyond the gate, near the **seats of the choir**, inlaid and carved by Domenico Capra senior (? -1591) and finished by Gabriele Capra junior in 1603.

If on the one hand the originality of the architectonic setting created by Antonio Campi for this fresco is surprising, on the other his skill in mixing a mannered classicism with many naturalistic characteristics typical of the most pure Lombard tradition is also striking. The evangelical subject is therefore freed from every historical and doctrinal reference and becomes humanized and contemporary. Also to be mentioned is the static **Christ's Baptism** frescoed by Campi on the opposite wall. From that whispering

St. Sigismund's: 1.-2. Chapel of St. John the Baptist. Frescoes with episodes from the life of the Baptist, by A. Campi; 3. St. John the Baptist's Chapel: Salome, by A. Campi.

3

groups of white-dressed Angels, their robes the only merry note in the whole scene, the painter, following his rich inventiveness, isolated two of them, represented in the act of falling headlong from the cyma into the gloomy prison where the Baptist lies in the paleness of death. Two very refined *stucco medallions* modelled by the artist below the frescoes also refer to the life of Christ's Forerunner and represent: **Herod's banquet**, the first on the left and **John the Baptist in prison, visited by his disciples** on the right. Past the third *chapel* we come to the one devoted to *SS. Catherine and Cecily* in which Bernardino Campi painted the altar-piece and the vault frescoes, together with the stucco worker Giovanni Battista Cambi, also called Bombarda, and the lunette above the cyma of the 17th century altar-piece. The other much celebrated altar-piece, contemporary to the one of the altar devoted to St.Jerome (1st chapel on the left), — they were both painted in Milan in 1566 — shows the feeling of beauty reached by Campi's exaggerated mannerism, always aiming at refining the most precise details and to show the most vivid colouring. **The two saint women, in their pink and light-blue mantles,** variously modelled in folds which are extraordinarily stretched and rustling, are washed by a rain of light which sweetens the shapely forms without creating rough shadows. While Cambi had worked at the vault since 1562-63 for which he had received several payments, the name of Bernardino Campi was mentioned only in 1574 which, therefore, could be considered the beginning date of the fresco decoration of the chapel, left unfinished by the artist and completed in 1667 by the mediocre Giovanni Battista Natali (1630-1700). The only danger in the plentiful production of Bernardino Campi was that his art could become fixed because of the repetition of figure in almost the same attitudes, like some small angels playing music similar to those painted in 1568 in the Nativity of St.Michael Vetere. In spite of his fruitfulness he was constantly looking for a new style, always wanting to reach perfection and managing to achieve nobility even through the barest technical instruments. Typical of this attitude are the four medallions frescoed on the vault and representing **episodes from the life of the martyr St.Cecily.**

The «Daybook for St.Sigismund's Fabric», from which the many payment notes mentioned above have been drawn, was interrupted in 1577 when the whole decoration of the church was almost finished: only seven of the chapels had still to be frescoed and they had remained consistent with the spatial unity of the original plan. However, almost one century had elapsed before the Hieronymite monks resumed the works for the embellishment of the temple.

The date which opens the second chapter of St.Sigismund's artistic history is of significant importance: the painter Camillo Gavassetti from Modena frescoed in 1625, in the last chapel on the right, devoted to St.Jerome, **the Viaticum and the Saint's funeral**. Forty years later, in 1663,

Giovanni Battista Natali signed and dated the altarpiece of the fourth chapel, on the left-hand side on entering the church, in which the painted **St.Paula on her death bed**, and frescoed on the walls **the building of the monastery and the funeral of that disciple of St.Jerome**. The herudite iconographical plan which had been predominant during the 16th century was replaced in the first decades of the 17th century by the will of the monks in order to celebrate the Saints belonging to their Congregation and the Saints of the Catholic Counter-Reformation: St.Ignatius Loyola, St.Filippo Neri and St.Theresa of Avila, all of them canonized in 1610. The chapels devoted to them lie along the right side of the nave: in *the first, devoted to St.Filippo Neri* worked only Roberto

De Longe (1646-1709); in *the second, devoted to St. Ignatius Loyola*, Angelo Innocente Massarotti (1654-1723) and in *the fourth, devoted to St. Theresa of Avila* worked again the Flemish Roberto De Longe. These works bear no datings, but their formal and colouring features suggest that they may date back to the last decades of the 17th century. Together with the desire to honour the Saints of the post-Trent reformation these works were also a product of the devotion of private individuals, like in the *chapel of the Sorrowful Mysteries*, completely frescoed by Massarotti between 1702 and

1703 (2nd chapel to the left) and in the one devoted to the *Guardian Angel* (1st chapel to the left). In the latter are to be found works by the three above-mentioned representatives of the 17th-18th century art in Cremona and in the Po valley: De Longe, Massarotti, Pietro Maggi from Milan and the Cremonese Sigismondo Francesco Boccaccino (1659-1740).

The last pictorial work which marks the very end of such a gorgeous gallery of local art is the one left by Marc'Antonio Ghislina (1676-1756) from Casale Monferrato who painted in 1725 two canvases in order to cover the rough frescoes by Giovanni Battista Natali in the chapel devoted to SS. Catherine and Cecily. The paintings hang now on the walls of the *third chapel on the left*, devoted to SS. Pammachio and Eusebio, disciples of St. Jerome who was also represented in the altarpiece by Carlo Picenardi segnior from Cremona.

The Hieronymite monks governed St. Sigismund Abbey until 1798, when they were suppressed; from then on the church has been established as a parish.

St. Sigismund's: *1. Vault and stucco works of St. Cecilia's Chapel, with frescoes by B. Campi, and stuccoworks by Giovanni Battista Cambi, also called Bombarda; 2. St. Jerome's Chapel: Transport of St. Jerome to the tomb, detail of a fresco by Camillo Gavasetti from Modena.*

The Stringed - Instrument Making Tradition

The tradition of stringed-instruments making in Cremona has always been one of the most peculiar features in the history of the town since its development in the first half of the 16th century. As a matter of fact not only are its worldwide renowned figures of stringed-instrument makers, from the Amati to the Stradivari families, still remembered for the artistic quality of their production of violins, violas and cellos, but also and even more for the influence that the tradition they created and kept alive has had, and indeed still has, on the stringed-instrument making world of all countries. The importance of the appeal represented by these instruments, and particularly by violins, for tourists, who have been coming to see the famous world of instrument makers from Cremona since the second half of the 17th century, is not to be ignored either. Although imaginative tales claiming that the instrument makers from Cremona had invented the predecessor of the classical violin were not lacking in that environment, it is undoubted that violins of the Cremona school were already very sought after all over Europe in the 17th century and considered first-quality instruments *par excellence*.

Violins produced by the classical Cremona school between the 16th and the 18th centuries are different from contemporary ones produced elsewhere in Italy and in Europe for their peculiar refinement of conception both in their overall form and in that of each one of their components. Moreover it has been proved that those which are now considered the best instruments, as far as the acoustic-musical performance quality they allow is concerned, always come from the classical Cremona tradition (although they may have been renovated or widely restored, mostly during the 19th century).

A classical violin from Cremona is usually made of very high-quality wood, both as regards the choice of the Norway spruce for the sound-board and the choice of maple parts for bottom, ribs and neck. The arrangement of the Norway spruce fibres is usually very regular and it shows particular translucent facets which build the so-called resonance spruce. Usually, maple components have also a particular look, made precious by so-called «veining», i.e. irregular spots in the trunk development resembling flames whose shapes change on the surface of the different parts. If we consider the relative rareness of such woods we can easily imagine why the classical Cremona production had particularly distinguished purchasers: Andrea Amati allegedly built instruments for the Court of Charles IX of France and Antonio Stradivari's making of a quintet for Great Prince Ferdinand of Tuscany and of another quintet for the Royal Court of Madrid are proved by documents. Count Cozio di Salabue, a lover and a collector of stringed instruments who lived between the 18th and the 19th centuries, although preferring a violin by J.Steiner, was also proud to have Cremona instruments in his collection. A number of notes and letters written by Count Cozio (1774 - 1845) and preserved in the Cremona Town Museum have helped in the reconstruction of events related to the dispersion of Antonio Stradivari's (1644? - 1737?) inheritance; in addition, besides a confirmation of the high repute of stringed-instrument makers from Cremona in the days of Antonio Stradivari, the Count's writings have also brought to light the unavoidable commerce carried out by unscrupulous traders in the stringed-instrument making milieu.

The most remarkable changes which affected the production of the classical Cremona school through the centuries and which were caused by the high quality ascribed to those instruments, were the renovations and modifications asked for by composers and carried out by instrument makers who, as reported by Count di Salabue in his notes, were often far from being refined craftsmen. As a result none of the classical instruments from Cremona has survived in its original state because the replacement of the neck, of visible parts of the framing (fingerboard, tail-piece, bridge and strings) and of internal ones (bass-bar and soundpost) practically turned instruments which were famous for their «human» or «silvery» voice (as they were still classified in the first half of the 19th century) into modern instruments. The varnishes themselves, famous for their transparence, brightness and colours, to which extraordinary acoustic qualities were ascribed, were consumed by the frequent use of the instruments and were gradually restored by new varnishings in order to give violins back their allegedly original bright look. The only Stradivari example left is said to be a viola survived from the «Medici quintet», and indeed the reason for its surviving is that tenor viols became obsolete in the late 18th century, a time in which, according to Count Salabue's notes, smaller instruments began to be cut from bigger ones and their framings to be modified fol-

---

1. St. Sigismund's: the door towards the cloister. It dates back to 1536 and its deeply carved surface represents the deeds of the Visconti and Sforza family, a work by Paolo and Giuseppe Sacca.

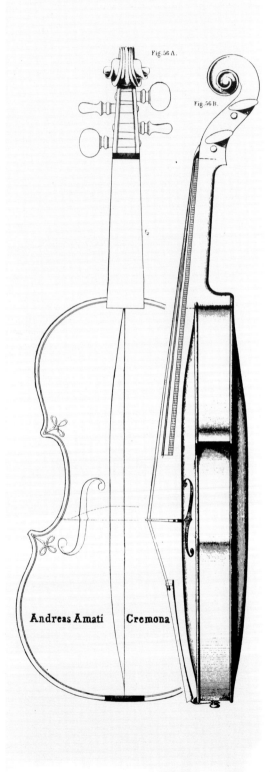

Fig. 56 A.

Fig. 56 B.

Andreas Amati   Cremona

lowing the French fashion of those days. This practice, still in use in some cases, is widely proved by bureaucratic documents concerning the re-making of the «Medici quintet» cello approved in 1877 and carried out later.

No documents proving the beginning of the stringed-instrument making activity in Cremona at the early 16th century have yet been found, but many believe that some of the original violins built around the middle of the 16th century by Andrea Amati are to be found among the surviving instruments. This is why Andrea Amati is considered the father of that school which, from the very beginning, developed products whose aesthetic qualities were far better than those of instruments produced in that period by, for example, the school from Brescia or from Bavaria. One of the instruments allegedly built by Amati in 1566 for the Court of Charles IX and therefore called «the Charles IX of France» is still preserved in the Cremona Town Hall. Others among the most important ones attributed to Andrea Amati belonged to the C. Witten II collection and are now in the museum of South Dakota University (U.S.A.). Andrea Amati was the founder of a school which was at first represented by his sons Antonio (second half of the 16th century) and Jeronimo (1548-1630) and later by Niccolò (1596-1684) who was responsible for establishing the style which made the classical Cremona school famous. This style consists in the passage from one curve marking the violin outline to another being so gradual

1-2. Drawing from: P.O. Apian-Bennewitz, Die Geige-Atlas, 1892.

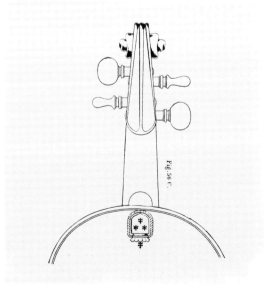

Fig. 56 C.

1

2

milies of stringed-instrument makers of all times and not only in Cremona: Andrea Guarneri (1626?-1698) and Antonio Stradivari. Andrea Guarneri was followed by several generations of instrument makers among whom were the two Pietro (1st and 2nd) and the two Giuseppe, the more famous of the two was called «Giuseppe of the Jesus» (1698-1744). The town of Cremona possesses masterpieces by Niccolò Amati, Giuseppe Guarneri of the Jesus and Antonio Stradivari, which are also displayed in the Town Hall. They represent now the symbol of the town and form a rich artistic wealth: in fact they account for what is held as the highest quality level ever reached by the stringed-instrument making from Cremona in its whole history.

The name of Antonio Stradivari recalls the figure of a man who is considered by many as the most famous stringed-instrument maker of all times. Violins attributed to him show aesthetic characteristics which, both as regards the devising of form and acoustic results, were hardly ever equalled. Unfortunately none of his instruments is now existing in conditions similar to its original form but the desire of violin-players and collectors of all times to possess at least one out of the several hundred instruments bearing his name is a further evidence of the high reputation of such pieces. His sons Francesco (1671-1743) and Omobono (1679-1742) were also instrument makers although it is not clear whether their production is to be placed at a lower level than their father's or not. As the three Stradivari died in succession in a very short span of time, the production they were working on was taken up by Paolo Stradivari, a nephew of Antonio, who sold it to several traders and partly to Count di Salabue. From then on — it was the end of the 18th century — instruments by the Stradivari, the Amati and the Guarneri families began to be more and more sought after and, together with others by different Italian instrument makers, sold all over

as to give an impression of harmony not to be found in the production of other schools. The same is true of the outline of the concave parts of the profile and of the «points» connecting them to the two main curves (the upper and the lower curve). The cutting of the sound-holes (also called «effe» in Italian as they are shaped like an «F») takes on a major relevance to the violin's aesthetics: the form which gradually came to be established is the one usually adopted by Niccolò Amati and characterized by more regular, often round «eyes» and less aggressive «cuts». The volume arrangement of the carving of board and bottom has suffered an evolution, although it has retained a constant softness in the passage from edges to the central part. Borders are always made out carefully and well shaped; the decoration is regular and junctions at the points are worked in a refined way.

Niccolò Amati was allegedly a master for a number of pupils, among whom were two who would later become the founders of the most famous fa-

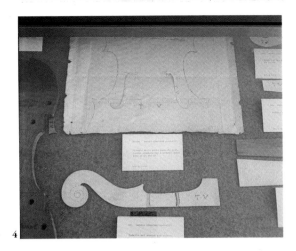

---

3. Form by Antonio Stradivari from which the «1715» was made. 4. Antonio Stradivari: drawing of the central part of the sound table with models of the bars of the two f's (sound-holes).

Andrea Amati: «The Charles IX of France», a violin made in 1566 and preserved in the Town Hall.

Antonio Stradivari: «the Cremonese 1715» ex-Joachim, preserved in the Town Hall.

the world through some of the leading French and English antiquarians. The number of famous instrument makers in the history of the classical Cremona stringed-instrument making is however much greater. These craftsmen, who lived in the age of Antonio Stradivari and were probably his pupils, contributed to spread the principles of the Cremona style all over Italy: Carlo Bergonzi (1683-1740) worked in Cremona; Lorenzo Guadagnini and his son Giovanni Battista in Milan and Alessandro Gagliano in Naples. The instrument maker G.B. Guadagnini, who worked in Piacenza, Milan, Cremona and Parma before settling in Turin, was entrusted by Count di Salabue with the care of his collection and the renovation of many of the most important violins of the classical Cremona school which belonged to his collection. At the time when Count di Salabue was writing his notes a number of other authors had allegedly already belonged to the Cremona school and among them he mentioned Francesco Ruggeri, also called Per, Gioachino and Gotifredo Cappa, Andrea Giovanni and Francesco Grancino, Vincenzo Rugier and Gian Battista and Pietro Giacomo Ruggeri, (they all lived between the XVIIth and the XVIIIth centuries). It has often been

◀ *Niccolò Amati (grand-son of Andrea): «the Hammerle», a violin made in 1658 and preserved in the Town Hall.*

Giuseppe Guarnieri del Gesù: «the Stauffer 1734» ex- ▶ *Zukerman, preserved in the Town Hall.*

material displayed in the Stradivari Museum of Cremona which also contains tools and curiosities from the classical Cremona tradition. The material passed from one craftsman to another and partly belonged to Count di Salabue's collection (like the pieces attributed to Stradivari) until it was definitively donated, among strong oppositions, partly by G.B. Cerani in 1893 and partly by the instrument maker Giuseppe Fiorini in 1930. The Stradivari Room in the Town Museum was in fact inaugurated on 16 October 1930, even though some pieces were only added afterwards. The present number of pieces, however, is sensibly smaller than the original one because of accidents and thefts which occured during the various movings and exhibitions of the collection. The bicentennial of Antonio Stradivari's death was celebrated in 1937 and on that occasion the Intenational School of Stringed-Instrument Making, now International Vocational School for Stringed-Instruments and Wood Craftsmanship, was opened; the Cremona tradition was therefore kept alive thanks above all to the work of the two most skilful of today's stringed-instrument makers from Cremona, Francesco Bissolotti and Giobatta Morassi. A number of instrument makers work now in Cremona and they all have studied at the School - some of them are now teachers at the School itself - which is attended by people coming from all continents. Several masters

said that the best production of the Cremona school ended by 1770; yet at least three more instrument makers are to be mentioned, who can be considered as the last followers of the classical school: Lorenzo Storioni (1751-1802), Giovanni Battista Cerutti (1750-1817) and Enrico Cerutti (1808-1883). To the last of these three we owe the preservation of much of the

all over the world. This tradition is characterized by the use of an internal form which is similar to the historical ones preserved at the Stradivari Museum in Cremona, around which, although with slight variations, the violin box is built. The neck and the way it is fitted, together with the remaining parts of the framing (fingerboard, tail-piece, bridge and strings) is obviously of the kind which became widespread in the second half of the 19th century. More recently a flourishing activity of stringed-instrument production in general has developed in Cremona supported by Vocational Training Courses organized by the Lombardy Region and a similar activity for the promotion of the cello production has also been initiated. Both at the School and in the artisan workshops the production of so-called baroque instruments like the viola da gamba, the viola d'amore and other plucked stringed instruments is beginning again. The teaching of guitar making is also promoted by a special Vocational Training Course. The cultural life around stringed-instrument making in Cremona is also enriched by other important institutions such as the Walter Stauffer Musicology Centre which works mainly for the specialization of stringed-instrument players but supports every cultural activity in the instrument making world as well, like the one of the Committee for the safeguard of National stringed instrument-heritage or of the Intenational Triennial Agency for stringed instruments. This body mediates the efforts of the most important Cremona institutions (Municipality, Province, Provincial Tourist Board and Chamber of Commerce) for the promotion, every three years, of the most qualified exhibition of stringed-instrument production from the whole world. In addition the Chamber of Commerce also promotes the spreading of the Cremona stringed-instrument market through non-business channels (like the thriving International Show of Instruments and Instrument-making Tools).

who obtained their diploma in Cremona have therefore contributed to spread the present Cremona tradition

1. Exposure of some contemporary Cremonese instruments to the sunlight during a phase of varnishing as it was in the tradition. 2. Master violinmaker Francesco Bissolotti and his son Vincenzo. 3. Master violinmaker Giobatta Morassi and his son. 4. Master violinmaker Elisabetta Giordano. 5 Palazzo Comunale: the room of the classical violins.

Marco Tiella

Marquis Giuseppe Zaccaria, earl of Maino (Cremonese benefactor).

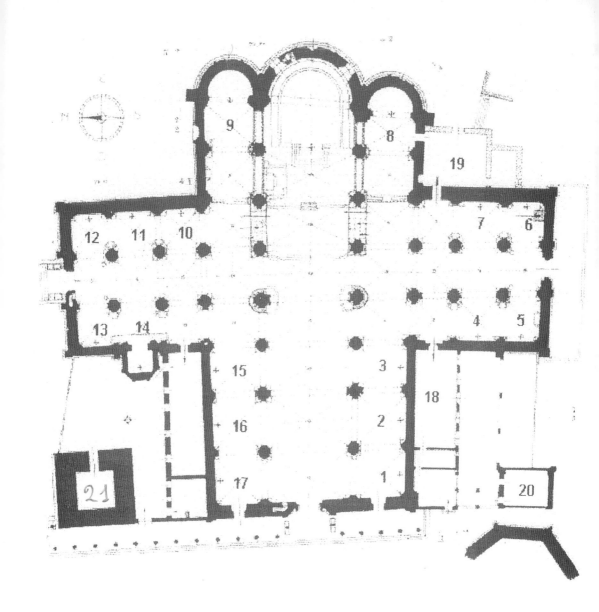

Plan of the Cathedral

LEGEND

1. Altar of Santa Caterina
2. Altar of Sant'Eusebio
3. Altar of San Fermo
4. Altar of the Visitation
5. Altar of the Holy Crucufix
6. Altar of the Annunciation
7. Altar of San Benedetto
8. Chapel of the Holy Sacrament
9. Chapel of our Lady of the people
10. Altar of San Michele

11. Altar of our Lady of Sorrows
12. Altar of San Nicola
13. Altar of San Rocco
14. Chapel of the Holy Relics
15. Altar of Sant'Antonio
16. Altar of San Giuseppe
17. Chapel of our Lady of the Graces
18. Sacristy of the Cannons
19. Sacristy of the Masses
20. Chapter-house
21. Torrazzo

Other details and impressive images of the Cathedral

1. Fifteenth-century view of the Cathedral in a marquetry of the choir-stall (see pages 26-27).
2. Foundation stone of the Cathedral (1107), Sacristy of the Cannons. Enoch and Elijah are represented together because they didn't experience the death.
(Genesis, 5, 24; IV Kings, 2, 11-12). They symbolize the eternity of the Church.

Cathedral (outside)

1. Expulsion of Adam and Eve from the Garden of Eden and the Original Sin (first half of the XII century); portico of the main façade.
2. Glimpse of the Major apse.

Cathedral (inside)

1. Boccaccio Boccaccino: Announcement to St. Joachim and St. Joachim meets St. Anne (1514-15), nave.
2. Boccaccio Boccaccino: the Birth of the Virgin Mary (1515), nave.
3. Boccaccio Boccaccino: The Wedding of the Virgin Mary (1515), nave.

Romanesque mosaics in an underground room of the Cathedral.

148

Cremona,
Discovering more details and images

1. Palazzo Stanga (via Palestro)
2. Palazzo Trecchi (via Trecchi)

Cremona
(Piazza del Comune)

1. *Palazzo Comunale (courtyard)*
2. *Loggia dei militi*

150

1. The "Minaret of Cremona": chimney of a spinning mill built by architect Luigi Voghera (XIX century), of Cistello.
2. Piazza Roma; public gardens; detail of a flower-stand.

151

The river Po at Cremona

Food specialities

The wedding between Francesco Sforza and Biancamaria Visconti (1441) and the Torrone origins.

The torrone

The origins of this sweet, almost synonymous with Cremona itself, date back to Roman times: according to old chronicles, some legionaries coming from the region of Cremona brought in to imperial Rome the custom of ending the most sumptuous banquets with a particular dish, a sweet made of honey, almonds and white of egg. More reliable information about the birth of the torrone, however, is datable to 25 October 1441, when the wedding between Bianca Maria Visconti — the daughter of Filippo Maria, Duke of Milan — and the famous condottiere Francesco Sforza were celebrated just outside Cremona. The bride, who brought as her dowry the town of Cremona, was offered by local pastry-cooks a sweet made of honey, almonds and white of egg shaped like the tower of the thirteen century which is still called «torrione». Since then the dish prepared by Cremonese pastry-cooks for Bianca Maria has always been called «torrone» and, in time, it has become one of the most typical Christmas sweets, which is still today highly appreciated.

The mostarda

The Cremonese mostarda (sweet pickle) is made of fruits coming solely from Italy, mostly uncarved and significantly retaining their original taste thanks to a particular preservation system:

cherries from Piedmont, Apulia, Piacenza and Naples; apricots from Naples; peaches from Naples and Verona; citrons and figs from Calabria; pears from Piedmont, Trent and Emilia; plums from Emilia; oranges and mandarins from Sicily and pumpkins from Piacenza.

Pineapple is the only exotic fruit.

Production begins in June-July and, as some kinds f fruits, like figs and pears, are not yet ripe then, tne produce of the previous season, preserved in pickle inside plastic cans is used.

Recommended Shop

In the historical centre of Cremona, in Corso Mazzini, a few steps from the Cathedral

Creazioni Laura

An elegant and refined shop in Modern Style. Our boutique has the exclusive right for the sale of woman clothes and accessories of glamorous names.

PINKO

LALTRAMODA   SEVENTY

Creazioni Laura Corso Mazzini n° 45 - Cremona
Tel. **0372 27057**

APT – Tourist Information Agency

Former ancient chemist's shop, now office of APT of Cremona – Piazza del Comune (Portico of Palazzo Comunale)

Azienda di Promozione Turistica del Cremonese

Piazza del Comune, 5
26100 Cremona

Information Agency

Tel. 0372 23233 - Fax 0372 534080
info@aptcremona.it

GUIDE TURISTICHE

GUIDE RACCOMANDATE	LINGUE PARLATE		GUIDE RACCOMANDATE	LINGUE PARLATE	
BOTTONI MIRELLA	ITALIANO FRANCESE	0372-430340 338-7306006	MIGLIORE DONATELLA	ITALIANO FRANCESE	0372-35821 328-7245917
BORSELLA GIOVANNI	ITALIANO TEDESCO	0372-410644 349-3724679	RAIMONDI ROBERTA	ITALIANO INGLESE	0372-458296 320-4312297
BRUNERI DOLORES	ITALIANO INGLESE	0372-452620 347-6360435	SCANDOLARA COSETTA	ITALIANO FRANCESE	0372-451602 335-6848750
DUHR GEORG	ITALIANO TEDESCO	0385-885070 Fax.0385-49561	VERONESI MATILDE	ITALIANO INGLESE FRANCESE	0372-560577 329-1568386

Legenda:

1. The Cathedral
2. The Torrazzo
3. The Baptistry
4. The Town Hall
5. St. Jerome Church
6. St. Imerio Church
7. St. Mary Magdalene Church
8. Church of the Holy Trinity
9. Church of St. Michael Vetere
10. St. Abbondio Church
11. Fodri Palace
12. St. Marcellinus and Peter Church
13. St. Lucy Church
14. The Ponchielli Theatre
15. Church of St. Peter on the Po
16. SS. Aegidius and Omobono Church
17. St. Augustine Church
18. SS. Margherita and Pelagia Church
19. Affaitati Palace - Civic Museum and National Art Gallery
20. St. Luke Church
21. Raimondi Palace
22. St. Agatha Church
23. St. Benedict

INDEX

Exclusive distributor: Giordano Ferdinando
Largo Beccaccino, 10 – Cremona – Tel. 0372 31524 – 330 715935